Living with a Budgerigar

This is Frank Cachia's second book.

The first book entitled "Living with Limpy" tells the touching true story of a unique friendship between a man and a budgerigar who both suffered a damaged left leg.

Living with a Budgerigar

Owning, Understanding and Interacting with a Budgerigar

Frank Cachia

A Catalogue-in-Publication is available from the National Library of
Australia.

ISBN: 978-0-9941509-1-2

1st Edition

Acknowledgement

Very special thanks to Dr Patricia Macwhirter, founder of the Burwood Bird & Animal Hospital for her advice and patience, when it came to proof reading.

Thanks to the Burwood Bird & Animal Hospital for the use of the skeletal X-ray on page 15.

Contents

Section 1: Owning a Budgerigar

Section 2: Budgerigar Behaviour

Section 3: Budgerigar Interaction

Foreword

I've immensely enjoyed reading Frank Cachia's delightful book about the experiences he has had in keeping his budgies Limpy and Oz-e and the practical, first-hand, advice he offers to others who may be thinking of getting a budgie as a companion. This is not a 'how to train your budgie' manual, rather Frank writes straight from the heart in describing budgie behaviour and the unique relationship that he developed with his two 'best friends'. He advocates how others are able to use his approach for the benefit of both birds and people.

Who better to write about this than Frank? When I first met Frank he was severely disabled following an industrial accident, he was in constant pain as he underwent operation after operation to restore function to his back and legs and would struggle slowly into the veterinary clinic on two crutches. His beloved, cheery, budgie Limpy was Frank's constant companion through those tough times and the close bond that developed between them was sunshine in both of their days. It was an enormously sad time when Limpy started bleeding from an abdominal tumour and we were not able to save him. Not only was Frank devastated but so too were friends from around the world who had come to know them both through videos and posts on the internet.

'A budgie, a grown man's best friend?' you might ask. In my experience in over 25 years as a specialist companion bird veterinarian, what Frank described in his first book 'Living with Limpy' and now this new volume 'Living with a Budgerigar' is not unusual and will resonate with anyone who ever has had, or would like to have, a deep connection with an individual of a species other than our own. The age or gender of the person seeking the connection is not critical, nor is the species of bird or animal being befriended; rather it is the desire to have a meaningful, reciprocal relationship where both parties have choice, rather than just giving commands and wanting obedience.

There is a charm to Frank's writing style that comes of English not being his first language and he makes no pretence of having any formal scientific training so don't expect technical jargon. The advice he offers, however, aligns neatly with current academic thinking regarding 'force-free' training methods and the information he gives regarding care and diet is sound. While not everyone will agree with all of his suggestions, I'm sure old hands and new comers to the world of bird keeping alike will enjoy his stories and learn from them as they visit Frank, in his home, 'Living with a Budgerigar'.

Dr Pat Macwhirter, BVSc (Hons), PhD, FACVSc
Registered Veterinary Specialist in Bird Medicine
Burwood Bird and Animal Hospital,
Melbourne, Australia
July 2014

Preface

A budgerigar is perhaps one of the most rewarding pet anyone can ever have. They always welcome the sun with a dazzling array of colour and song. Their presence is contagious. Any person will always greet a budgerigar with a whistle and is overcome with joy if the budgie returns the mimicked sound. No one, who approaches a budgie, is capable of holding a frown, as soon as their eyes meet; this little bird guarantees to place a smile on anyone's face. He has the uncanny ability to project a look that will always touch anyone's heart.

Such a loving creature, few ever regret owning one.

Frank Cachia

ntroduction

WHY BUY A BUDGERIGAR?

Of all the pets available to own, the budgerigar must surely be the cheapest to look after. Other than some selected vegetables, a bag of seeds costing a few dollars will keep him fed for weeks. And unlike other indoor pets, is extremely easy to look after. Having evolved in the arid region of Australia budgies are quite robust. While flying they aren't exactly relaxing, the demand on their heart and lungs is high and this is what makes them quite hardy. Their ability to eat stale food, drink water that we wouldn't touch because it will make us sick, shows that they are far tougher than us.

To help you get the most out of your new pet it is best to first learn to understand him. Journey with me and I'll show you what "Living with a Budgerigar" is all about

I have had quite a number of budgies and in this book I'll be referring to my beloved Limpy, a budgie that saw me write a book titled "Living with Limpy" and my current budgie Oz-e. Because both Limpy and Oz-e are male budgies I'll be using the male gender throughout. It is not my intention to leave out his better half.

First things first

WHAT IS A BUDGERIGAR?

A budgerigar, usually called a budgie is a small bird. This small bird in its natural wild state, flies around in small flocks, however under ideal conditions the flock can easily grow in the thousands, certainly an impressive sight to see.

This bird is just as happy to spend its life in suburbia. Easily domesticated, their delightful outgoing behaviour launched them onto the world. From the bottom of the globe it has spread its wings and is seen throughout the world.

Wherever you go, whoever you know, someone always knows or knows another who own or have owned a budgerigar.

Purchased as a family pet or given as a gift, this chirpy, colourful and playful bird is owned by people from all walks of life. You'll see him with engineers, clerks, plumbers, labour and management. The owner, no matter what his position in life, no matter what his job is and however it may control his way of life is never happier than when anyone asks him how his budgie is. He delights, talking about the antics of his pet. For such a small bird he seems to take over the running of the household. And if the bird has chicks then suddenly the owner carries on and tells anyone who cares to listen, his budgie's behaviour. Friends the world over accept the owners' actions, partners are often affected with his enthusiasm and most likely, eventually are also taken in. The public accept him and wild eyed children want to spend time with him.

It never fails to amaze me how this bird asks for so little yet has the capacity to offer so much. His activities can be so comical and his antics so infectious. His ability to mimic humans both in whistling or speech never fails to fascinate anyone within hearing distance. Daily, without fail, he brightens anyone's life with a free concert, emitting chirps and whistles irrespective of whether he has an audience or not. Upon seeing a budgie, a person will always greet him with a whistle and is thrilled if the budgie returns the mimicked sound.

Countless photographs are taken of the bird, very much in the same way as that of a child's upbringing. Again as soon as anyone makes the fatal mistake of asking an owner about the bird, out comes the photographs and the poor man is subjected to countless hours of describing the bird behaviour.

Get a bunch of budgerigar owners together and the subjects will range from swapping food recipes, training of the latest acquisition, breeding, colour mutation and the raising of the young. Given half a chance these experts will even try to pass on their knowledge to their budgie himself, never mind the fact that he's been doing this for thousands of years – the owner's enthusiasm holds no bounds.

And those owners who let out their fine feathered friend out and let him fly around the house usually end up treating him as another human being. The beat of a strong pair of wings flying by, is music to ones ear and as he flies by the owner never fail to look on, following the flight path with the same look as that of a small child innocent gaze.

He'll sympathize if his partner has a headache or toothache but any change in the birds' behaviour, such as not eating or looking poorly, will see the owner drop everything and rush his feathered friend to the nearest vet.

When that faithful day of days arrives and the bird lets the owner know that the time has come to part, for him to move on, to cross the magical rainbow bridge up in the sky were food is aplenty and cats are banned, the owners' loss is staggering.

How can this little bird, such a small little bird leave such a large open wound to those humans left behind? A budgerigar's passing can actually bring a tear to a child and adult alike.

Such a bird, this little bird that has been given so many names around the world, also without fail, has the tag of "character" placed upon him.

As I said, the budgerigar, a loving creature, few ever regret ever owning one.

Frank Cachia

Section 1

Owning a Budgerigar

Budgerigar Features

B efore we go out to buy a budgerigar let's get acquainted with his features.

His scientific name is "*Melopsittacus undulatus*" Why does the scientific crowd make up such an unpronounceable name is a mystery. All I succeed in doing trying to pronounce that name is strain my tongue. The name "Budgerigar" is more than satisfactory. Incidentally the name came about when a white explorer venturing into the Australian Outback with an aboriginal guide saw a flock of birds fly by. Upon asking, (by sign language) what those birds are, the native in his own language stated a word which sounded very similar to the word "budgerigar" although most likely a bit longer in pronunciation. The explorer accepted the word and settled for the word "budgerigar".

Half a century or so later, when the white man started to learn and understand the aboriginal dialects it was found that the word the guide said wasn't the name of the bird but a word meaning "good to eat". Off course by that time the word "Budgerigar" was a well-established word and it stayed as the preferred name for this little bundle of fun.

Now, as previously mentioned, the budgerigar lives in the dryer open plain regions of Australia and can be seen either in small groups or in much larger groups depending mostly on the state of the land at the time, that is, when food and water is aplenty.

The Eyes

Starting from the top, the eyes have a pupil (central dark circle) and an iris (coloured) ring around the pupil. Understandably good eyesight is essential for safe flight. It is incredible to see how the eyes are able to see out in the distance during flight yet have the ability to focus at such close range as when the bird is practically looking at himself touching a mirror with his beak.

Their eyes are superior to ours. Unlike ours they can register close to ten times the images that we can. The eyes have four classes of cells which operate simultaneously. In the ultraviolet spectrum part of their feathers brighten so are able to attract mates. The throat spots, just below the beak in budgerigars reflect UV rays and can be used to distinguish individual birds.

The Eyes

With the eyes located on the side of the head this helps in providing a wider visual field than ours. (Don't bother sneaking up on him, he can see you far sooner than you can imagine.) This is essential not only for safe flight but useful for detecting predators. It is imperative that you know this because like most creatures of the animal world the budgie lives by only one rule "Fight or Flight". Now since he's no fighter then flight is his best option. So you must keep in mind that you should not carry out any sudden movement.

When you are in his presence do not make any sudden move as this will startle him.

If, for example you want the budgie to step on your finger allow him to see your hand from a distance and slowly approach him.

The Ears

Yes, budgies do have ears; they are hidden underneath the feathers. Located on both sides of the head, just diagonally beneath the eyes, the ears are simple holes in the skull. They are only visible when a budgie is soaking wet after taking a bath or when is heavily moulting. During their first days of their lives, young budgies don't have feathers, so the ears are easy to spot.

Their hearing is quite similar to ours, still don't bother sneaking up; he can hear you coming from quite a distance away.

The Cere

The cere is an area of tough skin above the beak that surrounds the twin nostrils. Generally speaking once the bird becomes an adult the colour reveals the sex mostly being blue for males and brown for females. When the female is breeding her cere slightly changes in colour and becomes crustier.

Unfortunately, just to confuse us humans this does differ in a couple of mutations (e.g. albinos, lutinos or pieds) where male budgies may have pink ceres but the females still have brown bumpy ones.

The Beak

I could write chapters about the beak, it is strong yet soft, sharp yet blunt; it is a marvel of engineering. It is made up of two parts, the upper and lower section. Both parts move, however the upper part, the larger part does most of the work. The larger upper part has blood vessels going through it therefore it is alive and has feeling. As a matter of fact as the beak is subjected to wear and tear it is continuously growing.

It is strong enough to be used as a 'third foot' when climbing branches or perches. A budgie can literally hang in mid-air using just the beak for support. Still it is soft enough for the budgie to use it to 'feel' any object it touches.

It is sharp enough to split a seed in two or draw blood from a finger when the person, for some unknown reason, inserts his finger inside a cage to prod the budgie. Yet it is blunt when feeding a fledgling.

The Cere and the Beak

Budgies do eat in a hurry so the seed is picked up by the tip of the beak, the tongue turns it around to the right position, remember no hands are used to assist, and the Tomia, the sharp edges of the upper and lower beak, are used to de-hull (remove the hard fibrous outer coat of) the seed. Small seeds, like millet are then swallowed whole, larger ones may be bitten in half.

It is truly a versatile tool.

The Heart

For a budgie that is able to freely fly about the premises it is worth noting how fascinating the working of the heart is. I'm not going into the technical functions of it rather, but being impressed by its workings. There's one reason why a vet will not take a bird's pulse--- he can't count that high. You'll be happy to know that while stationary a budgie's heart operates close to 700 beats a minute. In flight it is nudging a 1000 beats per minute. Very impressive figures to be sure.

When flying long distance a budgie usually 'cruises' at around 40kph. In an emergency such as avoiding a predator a burst of speed will see the budgie reach close to 55kph.

At those speeds it's no wonder I had just enough time to locate and focus on Limpy or Oz-e as either flew across the lounge room, dining and into the kitchen.

The Wings

The wings are elliptical. They are short and rounded, which is ideal for tight maneuvering in confined spaces. Observe a flock of budgies when they instantaneously turn quite sharply. These wings are perfect to use as a rapid take off or taking evasive whilst being chased by a predator. It is an absolute joy to see a budgerigar in flight as the wings make a beautiful sound and move in a complete arc.

Oz-e his wings perfectly formed about to land

The Rump

The rump is the area above the tail on the budgie's back. It is here that you will find a gland known as the preen gland. It is quite comical seeing the bird rapidly moving his head about rubbing the beak on this gland, collect some oil and use this over the feathers for waterproofing, cleaning and of course to smooth down the feathers.

The Vent

This is basically the budgie's bottom. A single hole that expels all waste, it is also used in mating and egg-laying.

The Rump and below it, the Vent

The Feet

The most common arrangement of digits in birds are with three toes facing forward and one facing back. The budgie on the other hand has two toes facing forward and two facing back.

It is incredible to see that the legs aren't just there for walking or grasping, they're a marvelous way to control the bird's body temperature. Out in the Australian Outback temperatures vary greatly between midday and midnight. Temperatures in the high two digit figures Celsius and then dropping down to bone chilling single figures aren't uncommon. So the budgie regulates his internal temperature through his legs. When the sun says goodbye and the temperature starts to drop the budgerigar reduces the amount of blood flow around the legs thus preserving body heat. Come midday and with the sun not showing any mercy, the budgie picks a shady spot, preferably with some breeze and increases blood circulation to the legs thus allowing excess heat to dissipate.

This is the reason why sometimes while a budgie is standing on one's finger, the feet feels normal and other times they're quite warm to the touch.

Two toes facing forward and two facing back.

The skeleton

Truly, a piece of superb engineering, nature certainly knew what she was doing here.

Apart from holding everything from falling into a heap, the skeleton is extremely light thanks to its hollowed bones. The priority here is lightweight and at a mere 20 or so grams that has been achieved. Yet it is strong, strong enough to be able to absorb the physical stress of high speed maneuvering and more important, upon landing. Remember he's coming to a dead stop from as fast as 20kph. That lightness is further enhanced by the design of the beak. As such, weight is further saved from the omission of a jaw and rows of teeth.

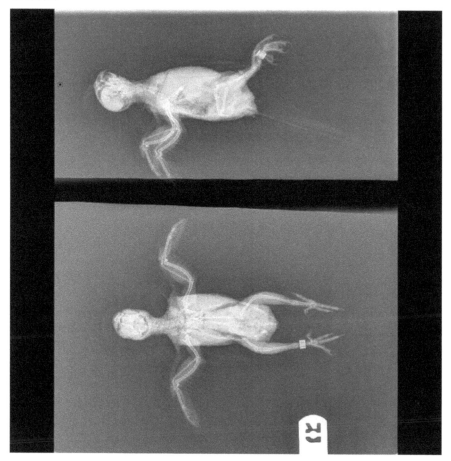

The skeleton

And finally the body's covering—The Feathers

The feathers come in nearly all combinations of colours. From the original green and gold to light or dark blues to whites, yellows, greys and any other colour mutation possible. The feathers are a budgie's clothes and they do an excellent job keeping him either warm or cool and looking his best.

They come in three parts, the down feather, this is perfect to keep the budgie warm, the contour is there to keep him in a waterproof state and finally the flight feathers, naturally their task is to keep the bird flying.

Since feathers wear out they have to be replaced. This is moulting. Moulting is seasonal. A budgie can moult once even twice a year, some budgies moult a little all year round, a couple of feathers at a time. But usually it happens at the start of spring/summer or autumn/winter. The first moult will take place around 12 weeks.

The first moult can be stressful because of the change to an adult. There's also a change as he loses the appearance of a young bird. You'll notice that you'll see your budgie spending considerable amount of time grooming his feathers; he has too, he must keep them all neatly lined up and in perfect condition. When he gets his new feathers the large, dark stripes across his forehead disappear.

During moulting the budgie does experience some stress. This is quite normal however, if the moulting is abnormally heavy and seems as if he's grooming far more than normal (like becoming obsessed about it) this might means that he's having a problem. Spraying him with lukewarm water every day helps him to get the loose feathers out more easily.

If he's really becoming obsessed it helps to carry out an inspection of the flight feathers. Place the bird in your hand, place the index and middle finger on either side of the head and tip the budgie on his back. Gently spread the wing, he's going to object but it is not hurting him. Take a close look at his flight feathers, in particular look for any signs of damaged feathers such as fraying. If the bird is picking on his feathers most likely the new feathers are having trouble coming out to replace the old ones. Although you can help by removing the damaged feather it is best to take him to a vet. Remember the bird is most likely in pain. The vet should pull out any damaged feathers thus giving the new feather room to grow. The vet will probably give you drops to orally administer to help ease the pain.

If you see him shake his feathers he's not shivering, he's just fluffing himself. This action helps him capture air, placing it between his body and feathers to either warm up or even cool down. He does the same action after being released from being held, he needs to have his feathers re-aligned. Just like us, a matter of re-arranging ones clothes.

I mentioned becoming obsessed with over grooming. If you start to see that he's starting to tear the feathers, actually pulling them out, that is clearly a sign of a problem. Stress is the main cause for this action. Don't waste time, he needs to be taken to an avian vet where not only will he be placed on medication but questions are raised to see what caused such destructive behaviour.

Buying a Budgerigar

The time has come to buy a budgerigar. But before you buy there are a number of questions that must be asked so as to make sure you make the right choice.

Do not make the mistake that a budgie is just a child's pet; a budgie is just as much a companion for an adult.

Ask yourself;

1. Do you want just a single budgerigar or more?
2. Is he going to be a pet or a companion?
3. Are you planning to breed?
4. Are you going to place the bird in a cage, aviary or let them fly around the house?
5. Does one select a breeder or a pet store or private sale?
6. Which budgie is the right one?

If all you want is a single budgie then it is a matter of going to either a breeder or a pet store and buys the bird. Private sales unless you know the seller should be avoided. Listen carefully to why the bird is up for sale. Some of the reasons or excuses require more explanations; be wary.

If the budgerigar that you chose still has stripes on its forehead, then that means that the budgerigar is still quite young. Those stripes will disappear within 6 or so months. Placed in a cage the budgie will soon settle down and spends the day amusing itself and being a delight to any observer with some unique behaviour. This is also the best age to train getting onto ones finger.

If you're going to buy more than one budgerigar then once again it is a matter of visiting either the breeder or the pet shop. One opinion is that you should buy a minimum of two so as they can keep each other company. It is best to get either two males, or a male and a female. There's a better interaction because if you select two females (hens) all they'll do is just sit at either end of the cage looking suspiciously at each other. Two or more males are far friendlier, cheerful chirping and their antics once again will place a smile on any observer as they amuse and entertain. Keep in mind that it is desirable to buy a larger cage.

If you do plan to breed them then you must make sure that both birds are over 12 months old. In actual fact it is best that the female (the hen) is around 18 months old. It is best to start with a larger cage and add a solid wooden nesting box attached on the outside of the cage. A straw base or wood shavings helps with comfort and insulation. Mineral and calcium blocks helps immensely towards better stronger eggs. It is also ideal to reduce the noise/disturbance level just before and after the eggs are laid.

Cages come in different sizes ranging from the humblest model to the multi-story apartment.

Ideal to use as a transport cage but not for a budgie to live in

The lavish up market models come furnished with seed and water holders, Saturday afternoon bath tubs, a piece of twisted rope hanging in a cage used as a swinging perch (also known as a boing) a swing, bells and revolving mirrors, plus a few perches and ladders strategically placed. By the time you add toys, a cuttlebone and anything else to keep the bird amused there's hardly any flying room left.

Large cages but hardly any room for flight. Budgies fly across, not up and down

So as a guide it is best to select an appropriate sized cage. The larger it is, the better it is for your budgerigar. Practically most cages would suffice but please ensure that 300mm by 250mm by 300mm is the minimum for one or two Budgies. Off course bigger is better. The more space available the happier your bird will be. Being able to spread his wings and fly about helps strengthen the wing and body muscles. Higher level of activity will see the bird in better physical shape. You too will enjoy him flying around. Stay away from wicker or bamboo cages. It wouldn't take long for the little darling to quickly chew his way out.

A word of caution; some cages have the door lifting up to open as in the above photograph. These doors are known as guillotine doors. Believe it or not budgies are quite observant and in time will tend to try to lift and then slide through them. When that happens there's the very real danger that they'll get their heads caught. I strongly suggest that the door be made secured by placing a clothes peg or any similar item to ensure that the door remains shut.

If you are fortunate to find the right cage and it is a second hand one buy it but before you introduce your new bird to it wash it thoroughly. First use the garden hose under high pressure followed by thoroughly scrubbing it from top to bottom. Do not use any detergent or bleach, soap and hot water is satisfactory.

An alternative is to build an aviary. This can be quite large. Unlike a cage an aviary allows birds a much larger living space where they can safely fly about. An aviary has enough space to not only put in all the conveniences of home but also contain plants and shrubbery and even a few branches to simulate a natural environment. The only problem that an aviary has is that it takes up quite a lot of space. Some aviaries take up a whole room. This can be overcome by placing it outside but then you will not see the birds as often and they are subjected to all sorts of weather. Worse than that, an outside aviary will attract predators such as cats. Under that type of stress no budgie is going to enjoy good health.

The only other option is to let the budgie fly about the house. This does create a set of unique problems but once solved you'll enjoy the ultimate pleasure of seeing and also hearing a pair of healthy wings fly by. The joy of seeing a bird in flight at such close proximity is one sight never forgotten.

He used to live in the guest bathroom before moving to the kitchen. He'll have trouble sleeping anywhere else now as the ticking of the kitchen clock and the fridge switching itself on and off has become part of his life.

Buying from a breeder or a pet store? This is more a matter of personal taste. Before you even look at the budgie, look around. Ask yourself these questions; is the place clean and tidy or in a mess? Are tools such as pots and pans neatly stored or are they all over the place? Are the aviaries or cages clean or do they need cleaning? As a final point a quick inspection of the feed and water should tell you the condition of the birds.

Oz-e coming in for a landing

No cage here, Oz-e at home on his favorite perch.

If the area is a mess then clearly the owner isn't looking after the place which raises the question—is he looking after the birds? If on the other hand he takes pride in the surrounding area then he's taking pride in the birds. Do not listen to the person's sales pitch, look, observe and let that make up your mind.

My first two budgies were Bluey, named because of his colouring and Indi short for Indian because of the colour markings under his eyes. (He reminded me of the American Indians, the way they wear war paint, under their eyes in the old Hollywood movies) were bought from a pet store. I loved them as equally as my next two birds, Limpy, named because he had a deformed left leg and Oz-e, named because he's an Aussie but spelt differently were acquired from a breeder. In my case I was fortunate because the breeder is a second cousin. The only extra information I received from the breeder was the date the birds were hatched. From both sources I received excellent service.

Quite often it's the colour pattern that is the reason for making the selection. Let's face it, the budgie looks beautiful or attractive and thus the decision is quite easily reached. But before you eagerly point a finger, you should 'inspect' the bird. By inspect I mean you should carefully examine the bird for any signs of sickness.

To do this you must spend quite some time looking at the budgie. I mean after all if he's asleep you can't exactly observe him at his best.

1. Is the bird active? If he's just sitting still he might be resting but then again if his breathing is fast yet he hasn't been flying then why is it so, what's wrong.
2. The same applies if while sitting still his feathers look a mess. If he's sitting on a perch and preening himself then that's OK.
3. Seeing him fly about, eating and drinking is also a sign of good health however if he has droppings around the vent that could also be a warning sign. One can't help wonder whether the vent is blocked.
4. Finally, if he's sitting quiet and "fluffed", then be aware, the bird may have health problems.

So in a nutshell if the bird passes these requirements, that is being active, chirpy, has a streamlined looking body and is eating and drinking then the choice is easy, select him and you've just entered the wonderful world of budgerigars.

Before you actually physically hand over a fistful of dollars it pays to ask the seller a couple of questions

- Are you qualified to sell birds?
- Where did you get this bird from? (obviously this doesn't apply to a breeder)
- How old is this bird?
- Are you aware of any problems, health wise, past or present?
- Has he shown any behavioural problems?
- What type of seeds and any other food has he been fed?

These may sound rather strange but it is best to get as big a picture of the budgie as possible.

Once you're completely satisfied then smile and buy the budgie.

Unless you have brought a cage along, the pet store or breeder will give you a small transport cardboard box. Being placed in such a confined space plus the movement in the transportation period will cause the bird to stress so don't detour, go straight home.

Daily Tasks

Now that you have a pet, you must keep looking after him, he is your responsibility. Looking after him should be a pleasure not a chore.

Upon arriving home there are a number of things that should take place.

1. Transfer the budgie to his new home (cage)
2. Select a spot where the cage isn't in a draughty area or worse, constant direct sunlight.
3. Make sure of the selected spot because moving the cage to different locations will subject the budgie to unnecessary stress.
4. Now cover half the cage with a cloth and let him be. He needs time to settle in.

Warning

Of all the rooms in an abode, the kitchen is the last room to place a cage. It's lovely to have a bird merrily chirping away keeping you company while you cook; the problem is the items used. Not so much the item itself but the fumes they release when being in use. Many kitchen products such as frying pans, toasters, toaster ovens, waffle irons, bread makers and ovens have a Teflon coating. The fumes emanating from these items are deadly to budgerigars. A budgie would die within minutes of someone using the self-cleaning option on the oven. Fumes from burning butter are also very dangerous, that acrid smoke can kill them.

Ironically, my first two budgies, Bluey, Indi and my current bird Oz-e live in the kitchen. Fortunately all my cookware is stainless-steel. As far as I know aluminium, copper, glass, corning ware, and cast iron are okay.

Incidentally cigarette smoke harms both you and your bird's health.

Feed

Budgies are seed eaters but that is hardly a good stable diet. A seed only diet is low in Vitamin A, D3, E, K, biotin, folic acid, choline, niacin, calcium, selenium, iron, iodine, lysine, methionine and fibre and other minerals and vitamins. When feeding seed look for and give the brands that have the little green granules that contain these supplements and also offer green & yellow vegetables. There are around 30 ingredients needed to keep birds in good health.

Play it safe, ask the pet store or the breeder what your new budgie was given. This is the easiest way because any other food that's not familiar will result in the budgie shying away from it. Budgerigars are notoriously wary of new foods. Even after a few weeks they still view the new item with mistrusting eyes. They might and I stress this point, might come around, but don't hold your breath. "Canary Plain" is a seed that budgies enjoy. If introduced early enough some budgies do eat greens such as broccoli, peas, silver beet and spinach.

A word in an avian vet will further help and educate you in what minerals and vitamins should complement the feed. I personally give my budgie a

"Finch and Budgie Crumbles" made by VetaFarm. This feed which looks like bread crumbs has enough minerals and vitamins to balance a feed.

"Millet Spray" is one seed that budgies positively love. They'll trip over themselves to get to it. Simply put they can't get enough of it, but it is fattening so go easy on it. It is perfect to give as a reward or as a treat.

Seed bells or seed sticks are to a degree acceptable but keep in mind that you're not in control and can cause the budgie to over eat.

Budgies can't process dairy products. Yet yogurt has some vitamins that are good but should be given very sparingly.

One 'feed' that should be introduced to the budgerigar is a "cuttlebone" This is the internal skeletal structure of the cuttlefish, a relative of the squid. It contains calcium and budgies do need it in their diet.

There are a number of feed containers on the market. I found that a plastic dish is a much more suitable container.

Budgies, when they are about to eat literally push seeds aside and pick up the seeds from the bottom of the pile. I place the daily measured amount in the dish and then gently shake the dish so that all the seeds lie next to each other. This way no matter how much he pushes seeds around none are being flicked out which reduces any mess, but more importantly, I can clearly see how much he's eating. I can also hear the tap tapping sound made by the beak thus know that he's eating.

If you use a deeper container it would look like there's plenty of feed available. This, most often, isn't the case. When the budgie splits the seed and eats it he'll leave the husk behind. The husk is the outer shell or coating of a seed. This of course is the remains of a seed and should be disposed of. It is far too big a task to separate the unopened seeds from those already eaten so every morning simply empties the dish and replenish it with fresh seeds. I use a measuring cup and the amount of seeds thrown out is negligible. Dump the remains either in the rubbish bin or throw it in the back yard and you'll soon have wild birds helping themselves to a free meal.

Overeating

As silly as it sounds a budgie can actually put on weight. A caged bird more so as the lack of exercise and boredom are the main contributors.

You must ask what the reason for overeating is. Often budgies overeat because of deficiencies in an all seed diet, see **Feeding.**

Where ever you got the bird from ask whether it originally was a bush budgie or a fledgling from a show bird as this does vary in weight. A bush budgie, in peak healthy condition weighs around 35grams where as a show bird usually weighs around the 50 grams. If he reaches over 50 grams he's starting to put on weight. If he's nudging 53-4 grams than it's time to put him on a diet. It is best to consult a vet first. Body weight is by assessing muscle mass over the chest muscles. Remember the vet knows more than you do.

If dieting is to take place this is quite simple. If he's with other birds separate him and place him in a cage by himself. Use a measuring spoon and fill one with seeds and place the seeds in the appropriate container. The following day see whether he has eaten them all or not. If he has, use the same spoon again but this time instead of bulging with seeds, level the amount. Once he's able to finish a level spoon then slowly reduce the amount again. Then go down to a smaller measuring spoon and so on. There's no hurry to do this, it's not a race, take your time. The budgie will slowly but surely lose weight. Once he starts to lose weight he will rapidly shed it.

Getting the vet to confirm it and to monitor the progress is recommended.

Remember that as he's shedding weight he will also be losing vitamins/minerals so place a mineral block or a piece of cuttlefish as a supplement.

Grit

If ever there was a subject that budgerigars owners argue about it is the use of grit.

A budgie eats by using the beak to de-hull the seed, then swallows it whole, leaving the outer covering, the husk behind. That's all very well but the seed is swallowed whole, there's no chewing at all, there's no breaking down the seed.

Shell grit helps in the digestion. Some seeds take a longer time to digest thus the continuous clashing of mineral grit against the seed will help the body absorb the nutrition. The grit stays in the stomach for months on end.

Eventually as it wears down it will harmlessly pass through the system. Once that happen the bird will ingests more grit and start again.

You can supply the budgie with some grit and let him decide. Only one of my birds ever had some and it was so minute over a 5 year period that I wondered why it was worth it. I removed the grit container and have never again offered to any of my budgies.

If you decide to supply your bird with grit, place it in a separate container. Do not mix it with his food. The bird chooses how much he wants and when he wants it. If he doesn't want any he doesn't take any. As previously stated some owners will argue not to use grit whilst others do so.

One must keep this in mind. As long as the budgie is a healthy one ingesting some grit is acceptable. But what if the budgie is ill?

We know that if he picks his feathers something is wrong. But what if the problem isn't visible to us? What if for some reason he's eating more and not just seeds, what if he starts to eat more grit, far more than the body could handle. This can lead to grit impaction. Believe me this can lead to serious problems.

Studies where undertaken in chickens resulted that supplying grit increases digestibility of grains by about 10%. As obesity more often a problem in budgies than the reverse grit is not essential for them. If they have a tummy ache for whatever reason some may overeat on grit and it can cause impaction – but this is rare.

I leave this decision up to you.

Drinking

Just like the food bowl, the water bowl should be emptied and topped up on a daily basis.

There is one other thing that should be carried out before adding fresh water and that is to clean it. Run your finger around the bowl. If you feel a slippery surface that means that the bowl has a layer or a coating of 'slime' and that should be removed. Although it is only 24 hours old, still water does leave a 'ring' around the surface. That 'slime' eventually will create bacteria.

A shallow water container

A deeper water container

Clean it by rubbing it off with a finger; if you are going to use any detergent make sure it is well rinsed. Then use a paper towel to dry the surface. You'll know it is clean because the surface isn't slippery anymore.

There are a number of drinking containers available. Normal tap water is quite satisfactory.

Incidentally speaking of water, budgies love freshly air rated water.

Hang on mate, that's my drink!

Second Last Daily Duty

Irrespective whether your bird is in a cage or has free flight the last daily duty is to inspect his droppings. This is extremely important, it is imperative that you understand and carry out this task on a daily basis.

Out in the wild a predator is able to know when a bird is either sick or ill thus this can lead to a possible attack. Because of this, a budgerigar has learned to hide his sickness; yes he actually masks the illness. Therefore a change in the droppings is a sign of a possible serious problem. A daily visual inspection of the droppings will alert you to the possibility of his state of health.

A normal dropping should be white in the middle and black around the edges. If that's not the case very quickly keep an eye on him. Firstly look at his food dish to see whether he has eaten all the seeds. If there is a small amount of uneaten seeds left that's not a worry but if half of the container is still untouched than alarm bells should go off. If within a short period of time there's no change or he looks worse off, than rush him off to a vet. There's not a moment to lose.

Watch out for the following:

- Watery dropping is usually an increase in urine output.
- Loose stools also known as true diarrhoea is usually due to stress, however if you're seeing it constantly throughout the day it is cause for concern. A sudden dramatic change in the bird's diet can also cause such a symptom.
- A change in colour or worse blood in the droppings means to hightail it to the vet.
- Undigested seed is the first indication that there is something wrong with the bird's digestive system.

Any of these symptoms is enough to go to the vet. There's not much time to waste, saying "we'll see what he's like tomorrow" isn't an option. For that bird there might not be a tomorrow.

Seeing a bird hunched over and or if he is quiet and lethargic are the first early warning signs that something is wrong. Another sign is if he's spending too much time at the bottom of the cage.

Once you get used to your budgerigar's behaviour, as soon as you see a change in his behaviour you'll be surprised how quickly alarm bells start to ring. The slightest change will place you on high alert.

With the lights dimmed so as to reduce stress gently pick up the budgie and place him in a transport cage and take him straight to the vet.

If the budgie is allowed to fly around the house you need to catch him. If the bird is ill he's not going to put up much of a fight so placing a cloth over him is a far better way to catch him rather than the use of a hand. If he's still able to fly away for best results a net is useful because it offers the least possibility or causing an injury. Nets are easily obtained at pet stores. Again if it is possible, lower the room light as much as possible, the darker the better as it doesn't stress him as much.

Once your bundle of feathers is in a vet's care there's nothing much else you can do, except worry. The vet can direct you to place medication either in liquid or powder into the bird's water container or to orally administer the medication. Surprisingly this is quiet easy to perform.

Place the budgie in the palm of the hand with the index and middle finger on either side of his head. This will prevent him from turning his head either side. By this time he's loudly objecting. That's OK he doesn't know it but what you're doing is for his own good. By tilting him slightly backwards it places him in a 'more submissive' position and he will recognise this posture which will greatly decrease his struggling. Before administering the medication turn the bird onto his side as this reduces the chance of medications going down the wrong way. Then it is a matter of just placing the measured dose of medicine in his mouth.

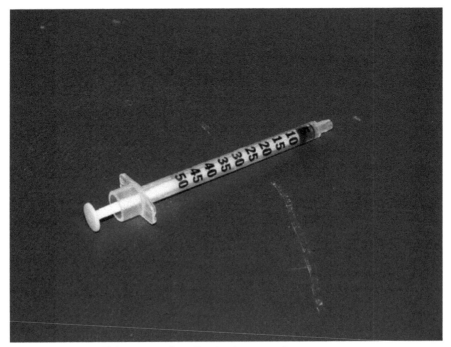

This measured application is extremely easy to use

Caged or Free Flight?

Now that food and water has been replaced, cage cleaning is the next task at hand. It is also time to decide whether the cage door is left open to encourage the budgie for some free flight. At this stage there are three options available.

- Leave the budgie in a cage.
- Let the budgie out for some exercise in free flight.
- Remove the cage altogether and let him fly around the house.

Leaving the budgie in a cage all day is the safest way to prevent him from any possible harm but that's as bad as having him in a prison cell. Birds are made to fly, evolution has worked that out. Health wise his flight muscles aren't used at all.

Cages come in all shapes and sizes, from the humble square size that hangs from a stand to the multi-story trolley mounted with all the mod cons. Unfortunately irrespective which one is purchased none is designed for flight. They should be long and wide rather than tall. Budgies fly horizontally not vertically. So keep in mind that any cage 'furniture' such as a swing or mirror should not be placed in the middle of the cage as this will obstruct what little flight space is available. It is extremely desirable to open the cage door and let the bird out. At first he'll fly towards the ceiling seeking height as a refuge. He will spend considerable amount of time there but that's ok. Eventually he will come down. Since he has spent time sleeping in the cage and most likely in the same spot on the perch he'll return there. That's his space, he's comfortable there. Don't expect this to happen overnight. The one thing that you'll learn about budgerigars is that they'll do things at their own pace. They are creatures of habit.

Whichever cage is used never place it on the floor or on any low position. The budgie will become quite stressed in such a vulnerable position. In such a position, he'll feel exposed, even extremely helpless. Budgies are more comfortable high up. You'll see this in action when the cage door is opened; he'll fly and gain height.

The purpose of these flights is to get the bird to exercise the wings in so doing it will help build the flight muscles and help keep the budgie in better health.

The last and best way is to let the budgie fly around the house. In my case I opened the cage literally within an hour of arriving home from the breeder and let the bird select his "space" in the household. As I mentioned my first, second and fourth budgie selected the kitchen whereas my third, my beloved Limpy, opted for the on-suite bathroom. Within a week I placed the cage in storage.

Final Daily Duty

Cage cleaning should preferably be carried out daily. Although it does sound rather extreme keep in mind that apart from dropping inspections, a bird stepping in his droppings could result in a possible infection. Therefore personal hygiene is a must.

When cleaning a cage, use detergents but make sure that it is well rinsed and dried as budgerigars do nibble/pick at certain surfaces. Replenishing the feed and water is quite easy and since most cages do have a moveable base, that too can be pulled out for cleaning. Spilled seed husk can be easily picked up with a damp paper towel.

It can be a bit difficult for you and traumatic for the budgie if he is still inside the cage so any movement should never be made in a hurry, slow and steady is the best way to go. Whistling or continuously repeating softly spoken words help the budgie be at ease. Select a simply two tone whistle and repeat it over and over again. This helps the budgie associate the sound with safety.

To a budgie an open hand is panic stations, because it looks like a predator's open mouth.

When retrieving the food and water dish always keep your palm face down. At the right moment, just use a couple of fingers to pick up the item. Whatever you do never approach the budgie with an open hand.

Pet stores usually sell a special paper to be placed on the cage bottom. An alternative is newspaper, which really works well and is cheaper. Keep also in mind that this does apply to a free flight bird. After all he has a sleeping area too.

The very final task is to pick up the 'down' feathers that are shed whilst grooming or worse when moulting. This isn't easy as the slightest air disturbance sees the feathers taking off in all directions. It is really worse while using a broom or a dustpan. So, it is best to place a wet paper towel on them. Once wet they are very easy to pick up. A hand held vacuum cleaner is a blessing.

Don't expect much chirping or activity in the first two weeks, the budgie is in a new environment. The budgie needs time to 'settle' in, to get used to its surroundings. Keep in mind that the budgie goes about by its own rules; he'll do whatever he wants to do at his speed not yours. So, never rush your budgie!! It will adapt on its own. Stay close to the cage and talk to it sweetly and quietly. Do not make any sudden movement because that will startle him. In time he'll soon get used to you. As mentioned, start whistling a simple two tone whistle, if you're unable too, make a soft sound with your tongue or whisper a word and repeat it over and over again. Not only does this helps the budgie associate the sound with safety, but also recognises you. Even before entering the room he's in, make the appropriate sound so he'll know that you're around. Seeing you will confirm it.

Since a budgie is able to mimic sound, in time, one day when you least expect it, you'll hear him play back the whistle. When you hear it for the every first time you'll look at him and desperately want to confirm you heard right. You'll make the sound again and when once again he whistles it, you'll be overjoyed. For the first time he has "talked" to you. Although all he did was mimic the sound, to you it gives you a wonderful feeling and you feel as if you can now start talking to him. It is the first sign of bonding.

Greeting your budgie every morning with a whistle or any sound that you have applied will soon see the budgie looking at you as you pass by. Within a relatively short time he starts to relax as he gets used to his new surrounds. Before you know it you'll start to hear a chirp or two followed by other beautiful sounds, some, longer lasting durations. That is another signal that he's settling in. Having gotten used to everything around him, he'll become curious and start exploring, including toys!

The basic 'furniture' in a cage is a ladder, swing, mirror, and a bell. A small ball usually with a bell in it is also a source of amusement for the budgie.

He's not going to climb the ladder but strategically placed will see him use it as an extra perch. A swing simulates a moving tree branch and he'll certainly spend time on it.

This is Oz-e who originally made the bathroom his own. He later emigrated to the kitchen.

Within a short time period Oz-e's naturally curiosity saw him looking up as if inspecting how the swing was held in place. For some reason he decided to climb the side of the swing. The lack of grip resulted in him sliding down, so, to regain control he flapped his wings causing the swing to spin around. When it stopped revolving it naturally started to reverse spin. You should have seen the look on his face. I'm surprised he could take off and fly in a straight line.

A mirror is one item that should be placed in a cage. A budgie will spend time looking at his reflection. To him that is very much like having a companion. What will completely surprise you is if you install a number of mirrors. If he is allowed free flight then introduce him to a number of mirrors around the house. His antics in front of them have to be seen to be believed.

Years ago I bought a plastic ball with a small bell inside it for Limpy; alas he never showed any interest. I re-introduced it to Oz-e. He instantly backed away but within seconds was curious enough to go and inspect it. As expected as soon as he touched it, it rolled away and he started chasing it.

Oz-e spent hours playing chasing this ball around

As soon as it moves the tiny rattle rings 'telling' me that he's playing with it.

Wherever I am in the house I could hear him. Once he actually tried to climb on top of it. He didn't succeed and slipped off. The funny thing was that he fell on his back still holding onto the ball. It's not often you see a budgie on his back with a rattle on top of him. He wasn't amused; he cracked it big time. He flew off screeching blue murder. I did what any responsible person does – broke up laughing. Wherever the ball was moved he followed it and not one day goes by without him playing with it, at times gently other times bashing it against any surface.

There are other 'toys' available at any pet store to keep him amused for hours on end.

The last two things to have are a cuttlebone and a small piece of wood. Just like a puppy that spends hours destroying a slipper, a budgie thoroughly enjoy destroying objects. A newspaper, cuttlebone and a simply small wooden block are perfect items.

The daily paper never lasted the distance with Oz-e around. "A well read bird"

Surprisingly a budgie needs some form of enrichment or activity of which toys are a good option. A natural branch for shredding is ideal to occupy his time. Birds are individuals, where for example Oz-e loves the whiffle ball, Limpy wasn't interested at all. His love was ripping up toilet paper rolls.

A word of caution; be careful which toys are presented to the budgie because some can cause injury such as having the head trapped in certain areas.

A budgie that's allowed out of his cage and thus is able to fly around the house is able to explore his surroundings. This result in the budgie experiencing more and will soon find other things to amuse him with.

Free Flight

As previously mentioned the last option is to let the budgie fly around the room or house. Each budgerigar is an individual; Oz-e is quite happy flying around the kitchen and dining area, whereas Limpy flew around the whole house. Flying the length of the hallway saw him "open his wings" onto full speed.

The sound of a pair of healthy wings flying at speed was only overshadowed by the blur as my eyes tried to focus as he flew by, seeing the magic of flight.

Nature gave birds wings for one reason – to be able to fly. That's not going to happen if the budgie spends his life in a cage. Flight is an essential part of his life.

I strongly believe that daily flights will make the budgie healthier, well for one thing it helps build up his wing muscles and strengthen his respiration and lung capacity and muscles. Flying also helps with own development, self-confidence, self-esteem, more aware and eventually even makes him a very social companion.

Free flight does present a set of unique problems but these too can be overcome by using common sense.

When asked why the bird isn't flying around, owners usually state two reasons. One is that the bird will leave droppings everywhere and the other is safety, meaning the bird will hurt himself by crashing into furniture, walls and windows.

Some owners have overcome this problem by clipping the bird's flight feathers. I couldn't think of how cruel an act that is.

First things first:

A budgerigar is a bird not an elephant, his droppings are so small that dropped on furniture or carpet will most likely not even be seen. The majority of droppings always occur wherever the bird is perched. In this case all that one has to do is to place a sheet of newspaper under the area that the bird lands on. If he lands on the top of a wall unit a small obstruction will see him land somewhere else. One can easily change landing zones. In the majority of cases the bird will always return to the food/water container areas as that is where he feels safe.

Any droppings on the floor, once dried, can easily be removed.

Eventually, having a bird on one's finger or shoulder is such a highlight of the day that the droppings on the carpet or furniture are practically the last thing to worry about.

As for flying into a wall, well that is unlikely, since his eyes sight is far superior to ours and rest assured that budgies do not 'drink' and fly. The only time any of my birds ever had 'an accident' was when Limpy came in for a landing on the kitchen counter. His undercarriage was stretched out coming in for a perfect two point landing but the smooth bench top surface was slippery, resulting in Limpy skidding sideways and sliding past me, crashed into the toaster. There's no doubt in my mind that he was not amused because a moment later quite a few irritating chirps could loudly be heard. I did what any responsible owner would do in this situation, do my best to control side splitting laughter.

Any room is relatively safe, but do look around and remove any item that might cause the bird stress or injury. A wall unit which is a distance away from the wall offers the slight possibility that the budgie fall and get trapped and unable to move. When that happens, you too will start to stress out. Other areas to be aware of that present risks are toilet seats up, hot fry pans, access to heavy metal and toxic indoor plants or fertiliser, ceiling fans even other pets.

When the cage door is opened for the very first time the budgie will always fly to the highest spot in the room. This is instinctive; height is the safest place away from any predator.

Very close to the ceiling, he can't go any higher

Leave him there, let him settle down, he'll stay there for hours. As a matter of fact do not be surprised if he stays there all night. Eventually he'll come down. Curtain rails will become a favourite landing spot. For the moment till he settles down let him land there. Later on if you do not wish him to land there roll a few sheets of newspaper, secure them with an elastic band and place them between the rail and the wall. They are out of sight; since they offer a soft unstable landing spot, the budgie will not land and deems that off limits.

Please ensure that if there's anything moving such as an overhead fan switch it off.

Flying in a confined space, such as a toilet or bathroom a budgie can feel trapped. In this situation if he's unable to land soon he'll tire and easily lose his flight speed. This will cause him to slowly lose height and will eventually either land or fall to the ground. You can prevent this from happening by simply closing the door. If for whatever reason the door is left open an open toilet bowl is a death trap. It is therefore crucial that you get into the habit of always having the toilet bowl lid in the closed position. The danger of a bird falling in can easily happen and once his feathers, especially the flight feathers, get wet he'll be unable to fly out and will drown in a matter of minutes.

Care must be also taken to ensure the bird's safety; nothing is placed in a position to cause him injury such as an unsupervised frying pan or a hot clothes iron. It isn't easy as the budgie once used to his surroundings wants to investigate anything and everything. Treat a budgie like a 3yo child, inquisitive yet unaware of danger.

I'm always asked how I prevent a budgie from flying into a window. Believe it or not there's an easy way to teach him.

Although letting the budgie out at night helps, it's best to just to block out the window. What I did was to lower the blinds leaving a 6 inch gap. Then cover half of that gap with cardboard or books. Physically place the budgie on the window sill next to the window pane and step away. Naturally he'll try to walk through but of course the glass will prevent that from happening. He will act like that of a fly trapped against the glass. Once he realise he can't get through he'll stop fighting. Then slowly raise the blind. Note: this can take up to a day or two. Unable to walk or fly through, the budgie soon accepts it.

All my budgerigars went through this exercise and none ever flew into the window panes.

Oz-e about to land on the radio

Oz-e, like Limpy, enjoying the sun's warmth, spends time near the window

Wing clipping debate can be quite a sensitive topic. The manager of the local pet shop isn't happy carrying out such a practice. He pointed out that close to 80% of people request to have the flight feathers clipped when buying a budgerigar. I said that I abhor the practice.

There's an argument that a bird outside the cage can fly out of the house or try and fly into a window pane. My reply is why the bird should suffer because the owner fails to close the front or back door. As for the window, just lowering the blinds till the bird gets used to the fact that he can't fly through solves the problem.

Oz-e returning back to 'base' on top of the fridge following a flight to the lounge room.

Parents with a little foresight and planning can make a house as safe as possible for a toddler. If this is so easily achieved why can't the same adjustments be made for a bird, why cripple him? If you want a bird to fly around the house simply make the house safe for him. Closing the toilet lids is the first priority. Make sure that the windows are closed or just ajar. The same can be said for the outside doors, keep them closed. If the owner does want to leave the door open to let fresh air in than install a fly wire screen or a security door. The placing of dangling plastic strips where a person can go in or out but a bird will never fly through is also another possibility. You can see these strips at restaurants or any establishment that does not want to let flies in.

Wing clipping is quite stressful to a bird. Cutting flight feathers is to suit the owner not the bird.

Eventually after flying around, the budgie will return back to 'base'. He'll enjoy a snack, chirped and now time for him to stretch his wings, yawn and have 40 winks. Irrespective of locality and background sounds, he will not hesitate; he'll just shut his eyes and go to sleep. It is incredible that he's able to shut down with loud background sound yet is able to wake up hearing a barely unusual audible sound. And if that is surprising wait till you see how he positions his head. He actually turns it around resting it in the middle of his back. Now that is flexibility.

A moment after this photo was taken Oz-e was fast asleep

Darkness is now approaching, the day is over and it's time for all good budgies to turn in for the night. As dusk approaches, the budgie briefly become quite active flying as much as possible and loudly chirping before settling down for the night. This behaviour serves two purposes. It burns up energy to tire him and increases heart and blood flow to warm him up. Once he settles down if he's in a cage cover it however, do not completely cover it. Cover just over half of the cage. Allow light into the cage, complete darkness will positively freak out the bird. After all, out in the wild, even on the darkest night there's some sort of light around.

A night light such as those placed in hallways is ideal.

Another 'aid' is low noise. If he's asleep in a quiet part of the house switch on a radio but keep the volume down to a barely audible sound. For a budgie total silence is far more nerve racking. Even in the middle of the night out in the wild there's always some sound.

When I brought Oz-e home he originally selected the guest bathroom. There he was getting light through the window from the street light and I kept a radio switched on for months on end.

No need to lower the TV volume or talk in hushed whispers once he's asleep and has gotten used to the normal noises around the house he'll sleep through anything.

So from the moment you replace his food and drink first thing in the morning through to numerous chirping and eventually whistling, having a few snacks and the moments before he goes to sleep, another day has passed.

You have looked at, bought a budgie and given him shelter and feed. You are starting to observe and enjoy his presence. In short you now have a flying pet.

It is now time to start explaining certain behaviors before we move to the most important part of all – human/pet interaction.

Section 2

Budgerigar Behaviour

Budgerigar Behaviour

"If only we could talk to our pets".

I laugh every time I hear this statement. You see pets are smart and know much more than we give them credit. Every day, our pets spend considerable amount of time communicating to us. Unfortunately because we do not speak their language we do not understand their signals.

For example what does it mean when a bird raises his forehead feathers?

In this section I have listed certain bird behaviour which should help you in the next section when the time comes to interact.

A bird in the hand

As the saying goes a bird in the hand is better than two in the bush. Well that's not the case here. Budgies in general do not like to be held. When the budgie is placed in one's hands he'll loudly screech. He fears that the enclosing hand is a predator's mouth. Another reason for screeching is because to the budgie, human skin feels quite alien.

When a budgie is being examined, a vet will always hold the budgie in a toweled hand. This way the bird doesn't feel the 'alien' skin. This reduces the stress level and will shortly stop screeching.

Therefore it is advisable from a very early age to teach the bird that 'Mr Towel is my friend' so that he's not frightened to be held when being examined or given medication.

If the bird has strongly bonded with the owner and the owner is present at the vet's then the bird will continue to screech. The budgie actually believes that by doing so is sending a message to the owner to come to the rescue.

If that's the case it is one very good compliment being given to the owner.

Bathing

Birds love to wet themselves. No, I'm not referring as in urinating over their body, but rather as in taking a bath. Budgerigars are no exception. They use water to help make grooming easier, feel cleaner and even as a way of cooling down.

Introduce them to water by either indirectly spraying them with a squirt bottle or place a shallow dish next to their drinking water. His contour feathers will keep him in a waterproof state. Although once wet he's not going to "catch a cold" it is best to make sure that's he's not near an open window which can very easily create a wind draft.

The budgie will take a bath when he feels like it, there's no set pattern however certain 'moves' take place alerting you that he's ready for his big splash.

Usually he has a very quick drink from one area, walks around the container's rim and drinks from another area and repeats it again. When ready he will step in the water, crouch down and wet his chest then usually steps out again. Most likely he'll repeat this process by stepping back in the bath, open his wings and again wetting himself. Once he feels safe don't be surprised if he repeats these moves a number of times. Oz-e usually goes in three or four times. His record is eleven times. I couldn't stop laughing pointing out that whether he goes in once or eleven times the chest is wet, it can't get any wetter. What are you trying to do, drown your feathers? Would he listen, nope, he just went ahead each time fluffing himself and walking back to the end and steps right down again. He loved it, clearly he was enjoying himself.

If you look at Oz-e on You Tube you'll see what I mean - http://www.youtube.com/watch?v=xD74lhOxCvk

Clearly a deeper tub is required

Deeper still

Perfect----Oz-e reveled in this plastic dish.

Thoroughly drenched yet within a couple of minutes he was bone dry

Beak Cleaning

Once the budgie has finish eating or drinking the next step is to clean the beak. You'll know he has stopped eating when he starts to move the beak in a zigzag fashion caressing the beaks against any item at hand. This action help remove any tiny pieces of food from the beak. When you consider that a budgie spends so much time preening the feathers and cleaning the beak you'll definitely agree that to him cleanliness is next to Godliness.

Beak Grinding

Just as we grind our teeth a budgerigar will also grind his beak, in his case however it is a sign of a bird at ease with himself and/or surroundings.

Biting

As cute as they are budgerigars do bite but as there are two 'types' of biting. It is best to know and recognise which is which as the meanings are worlds apart.

Biting occurs either as an exploratory or a defensive act.

In the exploratory mode the bird will use his beak as the name implies – to explore. Just like a baby places items in the mouth, a budgie does the same by actually feeling the item such as a finger or a cage bar. It's his way 'tasting' the object.

Real biting is a defensive action. Fear, is a great motivator to bite as well as when one intrudes into his space. Let's face it, if you poke your finger at his body he will become quite aggressive-----more so if there are chicks or fledglings present.

If you are intruding and you're not welcomed his first warning is by opening his beak. That's not a yawn that is a warning sign to keep your distance. If you then continue to approach he'll start a rapid clicking sound. Next step he'll actually lashes out at you, from a distance, while still producing the clicking sound. If you persist in becoming a nuisance to him such as poking your finger between the bars then he can and most likely will retaliate and aim to bite. Well what do you expect, how many warnings do you want?

There are three ways to stop him from biting. The first and most obvious is to not place any part of your body within the beak's reach. No matter how bonded you are with the bird, allow him his own space.

Secondly if he starts to bite, gently blowing on him until he lets go is the best way to deal with it. It doesn't hurt him, but it interrupts the biting by being just annoying enough.

Thirdly is to actually let him bite. As soon as he bites there's the natural tendency to pull away, don't, let him bite, it is that simple. However, make sure that you present an area where it isn't easy to get a good hold. Instead of the tip of a finger present a knuckle, it isn't easy to get the beak around the knuckle and apply pressure. You'll find that he'll be unable to bite because he's unable to open his mouth wide enough to use leverage. Once he understands that his actions are proving fruitless he'll give up.

Also remember budgies will bite in self-defense. This is a hard bite as opposed to a playful nibble and a sign that the bird does not want to be bothered. As already noted, females bite the hardest and it is not unknown for them to draw blood. It is a good idea to back off when a budgie starts biting hard as nothing will be gained by pursuing an activity other than annoying the bird and that will get you nowhere regards taming or training.

An untrained budgie will at times lash out and bite. Using the principles of 'force-free' training, that is rewarding good behaviour, ignoring bad behaviour and arranging the environment so that the bird (or animal) is most likely to do the right thing and can be rewarded, does greatly reduce such biting behaviour.

Boredom

Believe it or not there's nothing more destructive than boredom. Being in a cage in a state of inactivity will see your budgie heading down into a depression that in its worst form leads to self-destruction. When it reaches this level, feather picking is the result. As frightening as it sounds it is worse when you see your budgie actually starts to tear his wing feathers.

Out in the wild a budgie will spend most of the day looking for food to eat and to feed others. Inside a building, in a cage where there's no possible encounter with a budgerigar's natural flying predators, coupled with a ready-made accessible source of food and water and unable to stretch his wings, boredom can quickly set it. Give a budgie his dues; he's smarter than we think. Budgies are lively birds and they need to keep active, they need mental stimulation. A budgie couped up, spending numerous hours just sitting on a perch with nothing to do will soon see him stress out and engage in feather destructive behaviour or worse self-mutilation.

He needs some sort of activity such as a toy or two to help him remain active. A strip of paper to rip up and eventually destroy and a chance to fly about will quite often turn the bird into an active, happy, chirping budgerigar.

Budgerigars are neophobic

Neophobia is the fear of new things. Place a new item in the cage or in his surrounds and weeks and weeks can easily pass before he approaches the item. So do not be disappointed if you have introduced a new toy and he's not playing with it.

I placed a colourful wooden object near his water, 11 weeks have passed and he was still avoiding it. Yet another item, a new mirror, saw him investigate it the following day.

Clicking Sound

One sound that a budgie makes and it is a rather unusual "clicking" sound. This sound is emitted when the budgie is upset. It usually happens in front of a mirror, meaning the budgie is annoyed by his reflection. Off course to him the reflection is another budgie so his displeasure is being projected at the other budgie.

For all I know he's probably saying "Don't just stand there, say something".

The other time when the budgie starts this clicking sound is following a warning but the intruder keeps on approaching the budgie (see Yawning).

Chewing

A friend was quite concerned when she saw her budgie chewing a perch.

Why do budgies chew? It is quite possibly that such an action is to satisfy their natural craving to carve a nest in a tree.

You see apart from using the beak for eating, budgies uses it to explore, feel their way around certain objects. Thus they 'chew' on items. This in turn causes those to enjoy nibbling on items that they can actually manipulate. Paper, soft wood and a cuttlebone are the desired choice. So if you see your budgie chomping away at his swing, do not worry, he's passing the time doing something which is quite normal.

There is a side effect; it helps them keep their beaks trimmed and sharp.

Curiosity

Given the freedom of free flight, a budgerigar with time on his side, becomes extremely curious about his surrounds.

On one hand he backs away even where possible hides, yet at the same time he wants to know about anything and everything. A contradiction?

Picture this. Oz-e is one top of the cupboards looking down at me moving about in the kitchen. I approach him ready to open the cupboard. He instantly backs away from the ledge. Yet as soon as I open the cupboard door he runs to the edge to see what I'm doing. He just watches me as I pull away and then approach the cupboard again. This time I tapped the bottom of the cupboard with a finger. He, instantly move about the edge running around looking to see where the sound is coming from.

Curiosity

Exploring

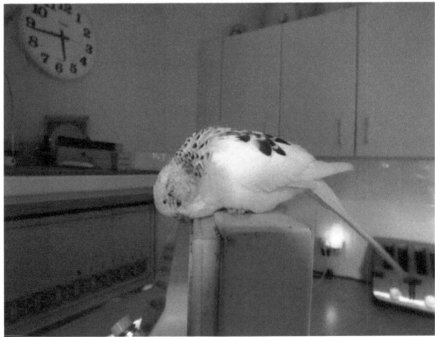

That's curiosity for you

Will this lead to an increase in intelligence? If a budgie is intelligent does he know it? How intelligent is a budgie? Unfortunately I'm unable to answer these questions but I do know that a budgie enjoying free flight will in time gain far more knowledge than one left in a cage. His insatiable curiosity will see him fly about examining every item or surface that he comes in contact with. He becomes more adventurous and will at every opportunity take off and broaden his domain.

Place him back in the cage for a day or two and you'll soon see a restless budgie looking for a way out.

Defensive position

Because of his nature to flee rather than fight a budgie adopts a defensive position even when asleep. If his sleeping perch is close to a solid object such as a wall, he always selects a position close to the structure. This helps him reduces the areas where a predator might be in a position to attack.

If you find that the new bird seems to be restless it is advisable to move his cage into such a 'safe' position. And remember once he settles down cover the cage however do not completely cover it. Cover just over half of it. Allow light into the cage, complete darkness will positively scare him. After all, out in the wild, even on the darkest night there's some sort of light around. A night light such as those placed in hallways is ideal.

Escaping – Flying out

You cannot imagine how quickly a bird can fly away through an accidentally left opened window or door.

If you like to have your budgie fly about the house and children are around and there's the danger of a door being left open, then place plastic strips like some shops doorways have will prevent such an escape from happening.

He'll very quickly gain height and speed it. Call him back. For him to respond it is more of an act of good luck then good management. Still do not lose heart. If it does happen there are a number of steps to take:

- Place his cage with an open door with food and water in it to encourage him to return and call out to him to encourage return.

- Contact Parrot Alert website,
- Inform your neighbours,
- Place advertisement in the local paper,
- Pass the word around,
- Place pictures of the bird on telephone poles, even offer a reward.

Ready for 40 winks and as close to the wall as possible in the 'safe' position

Oz-e is settling in for the night, the night light is on to keep him company

A person has the ability to return back home because, by using reference points, such as streets signs, recognisable corners and other road furniture is able to work out where he is. If he's unable to he can always as for directions.

But a bird on the other hand isn't able to reason the same way. While pigeons are excellent at finding their way home, budgies are not as adept. Once he has found his wings and is flying away he's just watching ahead and not looking around. The budgie doesn't normally take reference points to be able to retrace its flight.

So the first step is to hang a cage out with plenty of his favourite food and pray keep an eye on it. As painful as it is, yes hope, but don't hold your breath.

Familiarity

You recall I mentioned that budgerigars are neophobic, a fear of new things. Keep this thought in mind because when the time comes for you to change or move anything around it will affect the budgie's behaviour.

If for example you move the cage from one room to another a few weeks after he has settled down, he will be quite quiet for a few days till he once again familiarises himself with his new surrounds and re-settles. Even a simple change of a single item can affect him.

Oz-e spends considerable time on top of the kitchen cupboards. As such I need to clean the area of droppings on a regular basis. It wasn't easy as I had to tilt my head due to the proximity to the ceiling. To make it easier to clean I placed a small cloth on the area he stays on plus a paper towel further away so as to catch the droppings. The cloth was cleaned and the paper towel replaced when required.

One day I decided to change this set up and laid out a much larger cloth covering the whole area. From that moment on Oz-e flatly refused to land there. Three days later I reverted back to the cloth/paper towel arrangement and hardly had I stepped down that he flew back and started playing with his ball and wheel again.

Vacant Area

Occupied

Feather Picking

The day I returned home from a party and found Limpy on the floor picking off his feathers was one day I'll never forget. It really rattled me, worse was that it was late afternoon on a public holiday so I couldn't rush him to a vet.

Feather picking is a visible sign that something is seriously wrong with the budgie. It can be something very simple however it can also be a complex and challenging issue. This is where an avian vet becomes your best friend.

There are a number of reasons for such behaviour.

- Boredom----- imagine being shut up in a cage where the only movement is to walk to the feed or drink container. Lack of flight, lack of any exercise or any activity is soon tantamount to causing grievous bodily harm.
- Jealousy of a new pet makes the budgie feel left out. Believe me budgies are intelligent and pulling out feathers is a way of attention seeking.
- Underlying medical issues such as allergies, pain, liver or kidney disease, low protein or high cholesterol, parasites, toxicities or mental health issues.

Whatever the reason for such behaviour it is best to take him to an avian vet. S/he'll do a full physical examination and ask a number of questions to try to find out the reason for such actions and s/he may recommend blood or droppings tests or even radiographs. Based on the findings recommendations will be given for medication or changes in husbandry or the bird's environment to address the problem.

Fight or Flight Rule

Keep this thought in mind. At the slightest hint of a movement a budgie will fly away from what he perceives as danger. While you're in close proximity to him any sudden movement will see him 'reach for the sky'. Do not make any sudden moves such as raising your hand from out of his field of vision. This is of paramount importance when you start to interact with him. Let him see your hand slowly approaching from a distance.

Flying into windows

A budgerigar isn't able to differentiate between an open window and a plate of glass. This can lead to an attempt of flying through and the result is either a badly injured bird or a dead one

Although I have covered this, it is best to repeat it due to its extreme importance.

Before releasing the budgie from the cage I blocked the window by lowering the blinds leaving just a 6 inch gap. I then covered half of that gap with cardboard or books. Physically place the budgie on the window sill next to the window pane and step away. Naturally he'll try to walk through but off course the glass will prevent that from happening. He will act very much like a fly against the glass. Once he realises he can't get through he'll accept the situation. Slowly raise the blind.

Note: this can take up to a day or two. In time being unable to walk or fly through, the budgie learns to accept it.

Make sure to cover other windows and glass doors. I would recommend closing any curtains too. It's best to play it safe. In time he'll accept it.

Frightened

Do NOT forcibly take him out of the cage……...cage free time comes after the training is done. You can put one hand in the cage, with millet spray and go from there. Be very aware of the body language. If he starts to back away, pull your hand out of the cage. You are in his house and he feels threatened and that's what he's trying to tell you. He will bolt out of the cage every chance he gets; he's frightened and trying to get away. Keep repeating the whistle that he has heard so many times. That always re-assures him.

The analogy would be this. You're sitting in your house, something opens the door, all you can see is something that is 100 times bigger than you, poking this hand or whatever it is into your home and chasing you around to catch you......you don't speak the same language, this thing, this monster if you will, just took you from a home that you were comfortable in, perhaps you were in a crowd of those that spoke your language.....and now you are all alone...he's reaching for you, you don't know what is going to happen.

Would you not run away from that?

Forehead Feathers Rising

Sometimes a budgerigar raises the tiny feathers located on top of the head. Depending on the situation this usually is a sign of either becoming wary or alertness on one end or becoming stimulated, even a means of wanting to interact. When this does happen it's because he's becoming interested in something that is happening and is responding to a change in the surroundings.

One of the best tests is by being with him and whistling the same tune he has heard numerous times. He will mimic the sound and replay it. Now once he has done this a few times change the tune and instantly he'll stop whistling, raise his forehead becoming instantly alert, most likely will tilt his head as if he wants to pay more attention. This bird wants to learn. If you introduce the new tune he will in time joyously replay it back to you. It will never fail to place a smile on one's face.

Forehead Feathers Erect

Forehead Feathers Erect and Head Tilted

Funny Antics

One of the joys of owning a budgie is the funny antics that occur. It's like having a toddler; some of the action is guaranteed to break you up laughing.

Different mirrors bring out different behaviours in a budgie. His antics in front of the mirror can be mildly amusing to side splittingly funny.

An introduction to a swing can see either the bird just sitting on it or investigating it.

Oz-e has been flying around often landing on the swing. For some reason he keeps looking up as if inspecting how the swing is held in place. The first few times he landed on it he decided to climb the side of the swing. This resulted in sliding down so he flapped his wings to gain traction causing the swing to spin around. I just broke up laughing. When he stopped and the swing started to unwind it started to spin the other way. The look on his face was priceless.

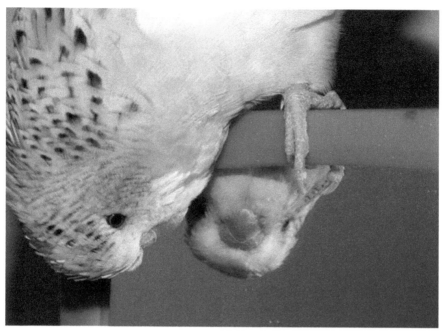

Hey mate, you're upside down

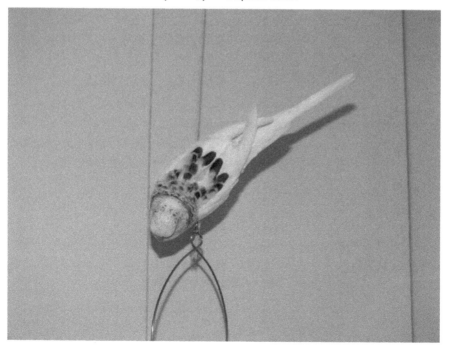

High wire antics?

Grief

If you have more than one budgie and one passes away, expect other budgies to feel grief. Yes they too feel loss. Those present will cease activity. For a period of time they will sit on a perch and stop moving about. Whistling will be drastically reduced, they'll go quiet.

In your case his loss will also create grief. Don't be surprised if a tear or two is shed. Whether he lived in a cage, with hardly a chirp being heard, or spent the better part of the day on one's shoulder the loss is felt. It is quite a powerful emotion.

Do not be afraid to cry, let your feeling out. It is a difficult period but you have time on your hands and time does help heal. I walked around like a zombie and shed quite a few tears when I lost Limpy. As time passed I remembered the good times I had with him and laughed at his antics. I now have very fond memories of a bird with a deformed left foot whose love, loyalty and friendship went above and beyond the call of duty.

Gaining Height

Even in a cage a budgie always select the highest perch, so you can well imagine that as soon as you release a budgie out of the cage he's going to fly to the highest point in the room.

There's a certain apprehension that he'll hurt himself by getting trapped behind some furniture such as a wall unit. You'll be surprised how quickly he'll find a spot out of reach or even a hiding place. To a degree this is good because he'll go there anytime he feels apprehensive or threatened.

First time I opened Limpy's cage he flew and stayed on top of the pantry and Oz-e stayed behind the largest jug on top of the cupboards.

Fear not, do not try and bring him back down; leave him there, let him relax and get his bearings and get used to his surrounds. He will be keeping an eye on you. Go about your business, sing or whistle, he'll be paying close attention.

The only thing that you should do is to place his water and food in an area far away from you. He'll see it and sooner or later will come down. He will come down but only in his own time.

Kept this in mind, the only way to survive in the same room with a budgie is to let him make up the rules. All you have to do is supply the love and feed.

Going away

Budgerigars are social creatures; they prefer noise to a quiet environment. Sooner or later as you go about your business they are going to be left alone in a house.

When you're away from the house it is best to leave a radio switched on to a music station. You'll be surprised how quickly a budgie 'joins in'. If possible, before turning in for the night leave the radio switched on, set at a very low volume.

Leaving a night light also helps. Remember out in the wild it is never completely dark.

If you are going to be away overnight leave the radio switched on and also another light in another part of the house. That way the budgie thinks there's someone else in the house – he hasn't been abandoned. It is also advisable to leave two days of food 'just in case' and inform a neighbour. If you're delayed he will not end up with stale food and water and a dirty environment.

Head Bopping

There are three reasons for budgies to head bop. The circumstances dictate such action.

At certain times whilst a budgerigar is merrily chirping or whistling he starts the head bopping as a playful sign. It is as if he wants to stress a conversation issue. Comical to watch as one can ask him a question such as "are you OK?" and it looks like he's nodding in the affirmative. It is also a sign that the budgie is a happy, healthy contented bird.

A budgie will also bop his head to attract attention to himself. This is a throwback from his fledgling days. By attracting his parents' attention he would get fed before his siblings.

The third instance that a budgie bops the head but not so vigorously is to regurgitate food to feed either the partner or a new born offspring.

Unfortunately if the budgie is by himself when regurgitating, it can be a sign of illness.

Human Food

A budgie that spends time on his owner's shoulder or finger will sooner or later be adventurous enough to tentatively taste some of the food that he sees his owner daily consume. In Limpy's case a slice of toasted vegemite bread was enough to see him fly from any part of the house and zoom in at full throttle on it. He positively loved it and couldn't get enough of it. Sharing healthy human food with your bird is a joy as you see him nibble on it. Certain foods are salty so beware, worse, some are deadly to a budgie so be careful and do ask a vet what human food is safe for a budgie to digest.

Some budgies are unable to process dairy food yet the tiniest amount of yogurt is good for them, just make sure it is a minute amount. Alcohol, avocado or any caffeine based food such as chocolate can be deadly so make double sure he doesn't get near any of these.

Inactivity

Generally speaking a budgie is a gregarious bird, spending most of his waking time being active with one thing or another. So when one enters a room and sees a budgie not moving at all, one tends to come to the conclusion that something's wrong with him. Before inspecting his droppings or calling a vet keep in mind that a budgie 'slows' down if the room isn't the usually lit area. This can happen when it is overcast. Budgies are sensitive to light. If storm clouds have cast a giant shadow across the land the budgie does become introvert and simply becomes inactive.

Leaving blinds or curtains drawn achieves the same result.

Independent

Budgerigars are notorious for sheer single minded independence. There's no way that they're going to do anything before they're ready. And even then there's no guarantee that they'll repeat the same moves. Every morning, when I enter the kitchen Oz-e walks to the edge of the fridge to have his first snack of the day off my hand. Half way through the meal he steps off, walks and looks at his mate in the mirror and then returns for the second course.

This routine can very easily change on a whim. He might approach me, then for no apparent reason will fly back to his perch and suspiciously look at the food in my hand. At times he'll fly straight on to my hand while other mornings he slowly, carefully approaches it. Never take anything for granted.

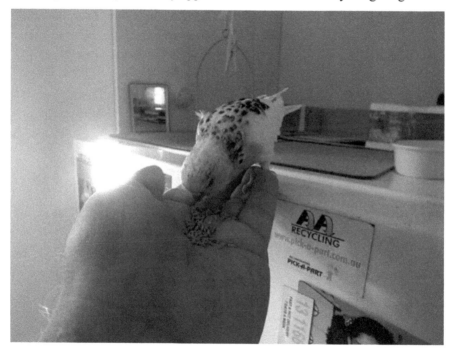

First snack of the day

And while we're on the subject of single mindedness the public believe that a donkey is stubborn; they haven't come across a budgie. You have to play the game their way.

This behaviour also sees the new bird's own personality come out. Each one is an individual. Whilst preparing dinner my previous budgie supervised me while sitting on my shoulder. My current bird does so from atop the kitchen cupboards. Washing the dishes one sat on my shoulder the other atop the kitchen radio above the sink. The only thing they agreed upon was to start eating out of my hand within a few days out of the cage.

Intelligence

They say that by your pupils you'll be taught. And this is the same where budgerigars are concerned. We insult someone by calling him a birdbrain implying that like a bird he hasn't got a brain. How wrong we are? As time passes in a cage and more so in free flight you'll see the budgie grow not only physically but also mentally. His individuality and behaviour sees him expand and increase his knowledge. The time will come that he'll do something so out of the ordinary that you'll smile as you understand his behaviour. Limpy walked up to my forehead and whistled to wake me up (whether I liked it or not.) You'll find yourself learning from him.

Introducing another bird

There'll be a time, usually after a couple of months that you feel or wish you get another bird to keep your bird company. This is ideal when you're away.

There's no problem whatsoever introducing another bird into the household, either just as another companion or for the first bird. However in doing so you must keep in mind that the following can and most likely will take place.

You are entering a threesome. The odds are that they will most likely bond with each other and you will be left out. Let's face it, why should one spend time with you when there's another of the same kind around?

If the second bird does bond with you, the first bird will feel left out and does start to stress. Budgerigars easily stress out. If you ask a vet about budgie behaviour one question always asked when a budgie is acting differently, is whether there has been a new addition to the family.

So if you want a budgie as companion that will bond with you, it is best to just have one. If this dynamic isn't important to you then having multiple budgies can also be enjoyable but expect to be part of a 'flock' and not necessarily your budgie's special partner.

Introducing new feed

As previously mentioned budgies are suspicious of anything new. This applies to anything and everything. Introducing a new feed isn't going to see the budgerigar rushing over and getting stuck into it. So it has to be introduced slowly. Fortunately budgies literally push seeds aside and pick up from the bottom of the pile. Very lightly sprinkle the new feed among his current feed. In this position he starts to eat it without being aware of the change.

The following day inspect to see how much he has taken and slowly over a period of days increase the amount and even decrease his current feed. By introducing the new feed slowly and under the disguise of his normal feed he'll start to eat it.

Use this same technique when powdered medication is required to be sprinkled on his feed

Leg Bands

When a budgie is hatched a breeder will attach a leg band. Usually these bands contain information for identification. Naturally these bands are extremely light and when attached are loose so as not to hinder growth.

Although it is highly unlikely that the band might snag on any object it is best that at the first vet's visit it should be removed. The last thing you want to see is a 'trapped' budgie with an injured foot or worse, a broken foot that is so badly damaged that it might have to be amputated.

Leg Stretching

Like us, a budgie stretches because it feels good. At the same time as he stretches a leg, the same side wing is also stretched. This helps keep the wing muscles and tendons in fine tune. It's a joy to watch him stretch because he's also demonstrating how steady he is while balancing on one leg. At the same time he's also displaying the wing colour pattern.

You'll also find that he flexes both wings whenever you enter his room. It's like preparing his wings to fly away at a moment's notice.

Show off

Medication

Usually once a vet releases your pet back into your care he'll give you medication to help with the recovery. There are 4 ways of 'dishing out' the medication

1. The easiest is dropping either powder or drops in the drinking water.

   Note; Because a budgie is able to go close to a month without having a drink this form of administering medication is always set for a long term period

2. Just as easy is sprinkling powder in among his feed.
   Note; Because budgies hull their seed there's the strong possibility that they may not consume the medication.

3. Holding the budgie on his side and dropping medication directly

in his mouth is next. The first time I tried it I was so nervous I missed and dropped it on Limpy's forehead, crown and ears. In fact everywhere but his mouth. But with a little bit of practice and a few giggles (he wasn't amused) I succeeded. The advantage with oral medication is that the exact amount prescribed will be administered.

4. Finally and again another precise measurement is given is by a hypodermic needle. Usually the vet will carry out this procedure. If you need to do it you may find this quite stressful initially but because it is necessary, with practice it becomes easier. Do not fret; the vet can instruct you in how to give injections if this is required.

Mirrors

As previously mentioned adding a number of mirrors will see your budgie acting differently in front of each one.

Oz-e has two mirrors and his behaviour in front of one is completely different to that of the other mirror

Mirrors, reflecting off the other plus the ball that he spend hours playing with.

The main mirror with a modified swing taped and used as a perch. This is also his sleeping perch.

Watching him in front of these mirrors provides hours of enjoyment observing different behaviours. He has no hesitation at certain times of the day to either "play" with his mate in his 'day time' mirror, merrily chirping loudly or tapping his beak against it.

The other, "sleeping" mirror he either spends time just looking or softly, and I mean very softly, chirp or whistle at his own reflection.

With Limpy, he used to fly around the whole house visiting his mirror mates in the bathroom, bedroom and two small hand held ones in the kitchen, one on the counter and one on top of the fridge.

He displayed different behaviour in front of every one of them. His actions in front of the mirror on top of the refrigerator were definitely different from all the behaviour in front of the other three. When I introduced him to this mirror Limpy would approach it and started to chirp and gently touch the mirror with his beak. At times the chirping was loud, other times at a more accepted level. But that changed.

Someone has to annoy the bird inside this thing

Just keeping you company, mate.

Limpy would slowly almost cautiously walk up to it, peck it, and then run away to the very edge of the fridge. It was as if he was trying to annoy that bird and then run away before he was caught out. He would do this numerous times. Then for reasons known only to him, he would again walk towards the mirror but this time go to the edge and 'peak' around as if to see the bird from the back. A moment later he would return to the edge of the fridge and eventually take off. He then, without fail, flew to the bathroom mirror and 'reported' his activity to that mate. It was one of the strangest acts that I had ever seen him carry out. This was repeated almost every day.

He was quite happy to just sit next to his reflection against the mirror on the kitchen counter. No chirping or whistling, no beak touching, just silently looking in or standing by.

Soft chirping or making faces and moving along the frame were the order of the day at the bathroom mirror. Without fail the bedroom mirror was there to argue with. Loud, boisterous screeching, taking off, turning around and landing once more on the frame and repeat the screeching. That mirror was made for arguing. I wished I knew what was said. Taking a guess I could well imagine Limpy saying "don't just sit there say something".

Visitors laughed when I told them of his different behaviour leading them to state that it looked like Limpy had a separate personality for every mirror.

Nail Trimming

While a budgie is stationary he's mostly propped up on a wooden perch with his feet in their natural proper position; wrapped around the perch. However if he's walking around on the bottom of a cage or any other surface outside the cage his nails aren't in the best position. If they are too long they can start to hurt him or get caught in his cage and result in a sprain, broken leg or even worse injury. They can also start to deform.

Just as we need to trim our nails, the budgie should also have his claws looked at. The choice is to either get the vet to carry out this minor task or do it yourself. If you want to do it yourself it is strongly suggested that for the first few times let the vet do it while you watch. This way you can see how it is done and see what the correct length is. He will also show you how to hold the bird and what steps to take if the claw starts to bleed.

Night Terror

There will be times, rare times, when a bird might experiences a nightmare. Well not a nightmare as we know it, but a night terror. A night terror is when something or someone passes by and casts a shadow over him. It can also be a shadow from a window that causes the bird to panic and instantly take flight. In that moment of panic he may blindly fly about and is likely to hurt himself so speed is of the essence to 'rescue' him.

As soon as you reach him, the first thing to do is to light up the area. Switch on as many lights globes as possible, flood the area. The lights, as bright as they are, will remove any shadow and show him see that everything is normal. A soft light is out of the question as it can and will throw shadows again, and that is the last thing a bird wants to see. Irrespective whether he's in a cage or not, grab him thus preventing him from crashing into anything. Holding and letting him feel warmth is best. Don't forget to softly talk or whistle anything that he has often heard before. His heart will be racing; he will be breathing quite heavily. It takes time for the breathing to return back to normal.

When Limpy and later Oz-e had had a night terror I did the following. I rushed over, yet carefully watched where I was stepping (remember my birds are not caged) and switched on every light. I picked him up cupped him in my palms and held him against my body. I softly spoke to him. Whistling the same tune that he has heard numerous times and my body heat helped calm him down. Letting him step onto my finger I then placed him back on his swing. Well I tried to, he refused to get off me, I could feel him tighten his claws around my finger.

Eventually he stepped off. As I walked away I kept on whistling 'our' tune, switched off the room light but left the hallway light on as this leaves an indirect glow in his room. By the time I went to the toilet and returned to check on him he was sound asleep again. I left the hallway light on and went back to bed.

In the morning it was back to normal, all thoughts of just a few hours earlier were all gone.

(Incidentally an earth tremor also triggers panic attacks—thankfully we don't have many of those)

No two birds are the same

"I keep thinking this bird will be just like my previous bird". Don't expect that to ever happen. All of them are individuals, there are no two alike. I bought Limpy (my previous budgie) a ball to play with. He never touched it. On the other hand my current bird, Oz-e, doesn't give that same ball a moment's rest. He pecks, kicks and jumps on it every chance he gets.

Noisy area

A budgie will chirp as long as there are other noises around. You can test this by switching off the radio/TV when the bird is chirping and he'll instantly stop all activity. As soon as you switch on the appliance, he'll start chirping.

If you have say, a group of adults sitting down talking and laughing in the same room, a budgie would usually start chirping along thinking he's putting in his 2 cents worth.

Given a chance a budgie prefers a noisy area. But if introduced to a sudden burst of noise such as a group of children rushing into the room he will shut up and will stress. This will not last long and his sheer curiosity will soon see him look to see where's the noise is coming from. An observer would see him darting his head around trying to look at everything and everyone at the same time.

The worse scenario is if any sudden movement or a child running to have a closer look at the 'birdy' is enough to scare him. Children should be educated not to rush over.

To a degree this preference of a noisy area is a blessing in disguise because if the bird is spending an abnormally long time just quietly perching, it could be a signal that not all is well with him.

Obesity

Yes believe it or not, budgies can and do put on weight. Boredom, stress, lack of activity and being in too small a cage hence unable to fly (or exercise) will cause the budgie to turn to eating in 'frustration' A deficiency of nutrients can also trigger an increase in eating.

This is one of the reasons why I let my budge fly about the house. All my birds look sleek, taut and terrific.

Whenever you take your budgie to the vet for a check-up the vet always weighs and make a note of it. Looking back at the previous record if he's putting on weight, even if you can't spot it, the vet will bring it to your attention. Ask what procedures should be followed to correct the obesity.

Dieting is the way to go. Follow the vet's advice. There's no urgency, this isn't a race; a slight daily reduction or a change of the feed would suffice. Have a chat to the vet he'll point you in the right direction. As I said the vet is your best mate when it comes to your pet.

Observation

You'll be surprised how much you learn simply by observing a budgerigar in action. Irrespective whether he's in a cage or not, his actions and body language tells you so much about him. Here's a few 'sign' you should watch out for:-

1. Chirping and or whistling ------------he's happy
2. Balancing on one foot-----------------he's contented or a sore foot, depending on how he does it!
3. Eating out of your hand---------------he's trusting you
4. Gently picking on feathers-----------grooming, cleaning
5. Viciously picking feathers------------stressed or in pain
6. Shaking his feathers-------------------trapping air to cool or warm himself
7. Hunched, looking bloated-------------sick
8. And the best one of all is when he regurgitates his food onto your finger------- he's feeding you, he's telling you, you have been accepted as his mate or he's sick, again like number 2 depending on how he does it!

Overheating

Come summer time and as the surrounding air warms up, we switch on cooling fans or air conditioners. Some budgie owners fear that unless they take this course of action their budgies will overheat.

This is highly unlikely as the budgie is able to redirect his body temperature through his feet. As the sun is warming up the air, the budgie increases blood circulation to the legs thus allowing excess heat to dissipate from his body. The reverse happen as the air cool down, he reduces the amount of blood around the legs thus preserving body heat.

This is the reason why sometimes while a budgie is standing on one's finger the feet feels normal and other times they're quite warm to the touch.

Keep in mind that the budgie's normal environment is the Australian semi-arid conditions. He's able to fly in double digit Celsius conditions and sleep when the temperature has reached below zero, bone-chilling, teeth rattling conditions.

Sometimes you'll be able to know he's getting uncomfortably warm when he pulls his wings away from his body. This usually happen if he's been flying around the house for a considerable period of time. To help him cool down introduce him to a water spray. Do not aim directly at him but spray an above misting. Most budgies love it and if he's one of them he'll look forward to it.

A budgie spends the most part of the day on one and even sleeps on it as well. In short, the perch is your budgie's best friend. Therefore it is best to have the right perch. The right perch isn't the one usually found in a cage, the plain piece of wood that is usually a pine one or worse a plastic one. The best perch that are available come in all shapes and sizes and are always found in a tree. Yes a piece of a tree limb makes the best perch.

If a plastic perch is the one that is being used please replace or consider wrapping it in a soft, self-adhesive 'Vetwrap' tape that helps the budgie gets a better yet softer grip. This tape offers a far better landing and the budgie is able to grasp it without possibly hurting the bottoms of his feet. It is very easy to apply, rolling it along the perch and its texture makes it cling to itself. It only costs a couple of dollars and is available at a pet shop.

Just cooling down

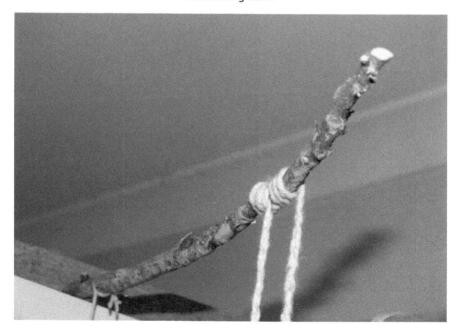

Perch

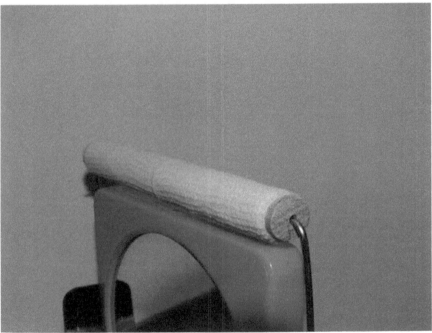

The tape applied to a pearch. In this case it is Oz-e sleeping perch

Physical contact

Once a budgie accepts and trusts you, physical contact follows. This comes through firstly by the act of stepping on one's finger followed by being allowed a caress and helping a 'scratch'.

When I have caressed my budgie's chest or either of his wings he just sits still and let me 'get on with it'. Very gently I move the back of my finger along the wings.

When it comes to scratching of the head this is also acceptable, as a matter of fact budgies love it but that's as far as it goes.

It is unfortunate some owners although meaning well pat a budgie on the head or back. **This is definitely not acceptable**. Birds will accept a caress but not a pat.

NEVER pat your budgie. He's not a dog. Dogs love to be patted. A dog irrespective of its size is able to absorb patting action onto its body. A bird on the other hand because of its size isn't able to. Yes I know that you will be gentle but a slight change in the hand position will make a difference. The slightest increase in patting with the finger can be harder than expected. Observe two budgies, they do not pat themselves they caress each other - do the same.

Preening

A budgie spends quite a substantial amount of time looking after his feathers. Lining the feathers just right, making sure everyone is in the exact position in relation to each other might look like being fussy, but that's not the case at all. Every time he lands he needs to re-arrange them. Collecting oil from a gland at the back of the tail, feathers are then re-coated and re-aligned.

When there's more than one bird present they turn and preen each other. Apart from the physical act preening is also a form of social interaction.

Quarantine

Owning a single budgie isn't a problem but if you plan to introduce another budgie then steps need to be taken to protect your budgie against any diseases.

This is when quarantining comes in. Quarantining the new bird is to simply prevent him from the possibility of passing on any diseases to your budgie.

Place the new bird in a separate cage in a separate room for a period of up to 6 weeks. In so doing, if the new bird has any diseases this time period will see the disease come to the surface; and will not infect your budgie. During this period I strongly suggest you take the new budgie to the vet. The vet will carry out a series of tests

A new bird exam ensures that medical issues which are not recognised by us can be picked up and treated. There are a number of tests on the droppings that a vet may carry out. These tests are for worm parasites, coccidia, bacterial or yeast infections and flagellates. Your vet may also want to take a sample of the fluid from your budgie's throat or crop to check for 'canker', or trichomoniasis, a nasty infection to which budgies are prone. Undiagnosed, any of these 'germs' can cause serious illness, weight loss or death if not identified and treated. Blood tests may also be advised depending on findings

Again I strongly suggest this. There's a great advantage in having these tests carried out and the visit gives the vet the chance to review diet and husbandry. Doing this as soon as the bird is acquired can prevent problems and heart ache further down the track.

But once the 6 weeks quarantine period has passed and your new budgie has a clean bill of health then it is time to introduce him to your budgie.

Bring him into the same room as your other birds but still leave him in the separate cage. Place the cages next to each other to see how they'll behave. Within a few days you'll know whether they're going to fight or get on well together.

Having overcome all issues introduces them to each other by placing them in the same cage. And from then on enjoy stereophonic chirping.

Incidentally, when adding another budgie, try to get either two males, or a male and a female. Two females (hens) will usually just sit at either end of the cage glaring at each other. With a friendly, little group, the antics of the birds and the cheerful chirping will never cease to amuse and entertain.

Regurgitating Food

To feed their young budgies regurgitate ('bring up') partially digested food. This is passed over and literally pumped directly into the fledgling's beak.

A male will also pass food to the hen this way as she's most likely sitting on a nest and unable to get food. Another reason for such behaviour is courtship, as a sign of affection.

With your bird it can be rather funny if you see regurgitated food stuck to a mirror; do not be alarmed, he's trying to feed his own reflection.

If he starts to offer you food by placing it on, say, a finger, that means that he's starting to deeply bond with you and may sooner than you think actually start to show signs of wanting to mate with you.

As messy as regurgitated food looks dripping down your thumb, feel honoured for that's one of two very good signs of a compliment that you can be given by a budgerigar. (The other is when he actually tries to mate with you, usually when sitting on your shoulder) In his eyes you have reached the top you're not just a mate but his mate. His complete trust and love in you is complete.

Scratching

Looking at a budgie scratching is rather comical because they scratch so fast, you wonder why they don't tear their skin off. It is one task that every budgie carries out. He absolutely twists himself into knots to reach and scratch a number of areas of his body. The most inaccessible part of course is the top of the head. So they bend the head sideways and use anything that comes to hand as a scratching aid.

Once a budgie is able to stay on you slowly introduce a finger to do the scratching. This is one act that no budgie will be able to resist. He'll positively love it. This form of physical contact is very much like preening, a form of social interaction. The more you are able to do it, the more he will like it. Don't be surprised if in time he actually lands close to your hand, moves near a finger and presents his head, approaching your finger for more scratching. This in turn helps the bonding between the bird and the owner

It's like a drug, for both owner and bird, the more you scratch the more he wants.

They thoroughly love it. If you look at Limpy on You Tube you'll see what I mean - http://www.youtube.com/watch?v=npjnHBQtaKA

Stop for Scratching Duties

As the budgie starts to trust you there will be times when he'll approach you. This pleasant act can, and will one day without any idea why, see him actually shy away from you.

Naturally this will surprise you and you start to wonder what on earth the matter with him is. Well believe it or not he might actually sense danger. Anything that might seem out of the ordinary, even something as simple as wearing a hat will cause him to back away. Even a new smell might do it. He might smell a cat on you.

Think back; have you by any chance been near a cat?

Lovely

Sign of contentment

When you see a budgie with one leg retracted, standing on one leg that is a sign of contentment. He feels at ease with his surroundings, used to what's going on around him and is totally relaxed.

Don't expect this to happen overnight. A few months will pass before you see your budgie at ease. As you approach him he will lower the other leg. This is expected as he has no idea what you plan to do, he's just getting ready to fly away. Remember his rule, fight or flight.

If, by the time you are within arm's length he hasn't lower the leg but stays as is, then he's telling you that not only is he at ease with his surroundings, but also at ease with you. He's beginning to trust you. Smile, he's sending you a message of trust.

Oz-e completely at ease

Sleep

A few very important pointers regarding the budgie sleeping arrangements:-

1. Irrespective whether the budgie is caged or not, his sleeping perch shouldn't be placed near a door or window where a draft is likely to be present.

2. The cage location should be placed close to human surroundings without being the centre of such activities.

3. Whether the budgie is in a cage or not he always settles down very close to a solid surface thus it is best to place the cage next to a wall. He selects this surface as a means of protection. This is to create a safe zone knowing full well that he's not going to get anyone or anything coming up from an unsuspected area.

4. It is also strongly suggested to have the cage in a position where he can see the whole room. Placing the cage next to a large piece of furniture can cause the bird to be startled when someone suddenly passes by.

5. If the bird is caged it is best to cover it with a cloth. The cage should be partially covered so that the budgie can see out. Total darkness is quite stressful. Also make sure the cloth does not have a strong smell of detergent since it may cause the bird to have difficulty breathing. Cover the cage around the same time every night so that your budgie can develop a routine sleeping time. If the sleeping perch isn't in a cage reduce the lighting of the room.

Irrespective of the activity or noise around him when a bird wants to sleep he'll just turn his head around resting it on his back, shut his eyes and do so. Do not be alarmed if you see him asleep at lunch time. He does this a couple of times during the day. As the sun sets he'll settle down and sleep through the whole night.

He'll sleep with or without any noise yet having some kind of noise throughout the night is quite comforting. To create the ideal setting a night light and a radio at extreme low level would be the ideal sleeping arrangement.

Remember that in the wild there is always a sliver of light from stars or the moon plus night creatures create enough background sounds.

In my case since he moved to sleeping on the fridge Oz-e sleeps directly under the kitchen clock and a short distance from the night light. I can't see him sleeping anywhere else because the clock constant ticking plus the fridge switching itself on and off has created a set of sounds that he can associate with. He's so used to these sounds that it has become part of his night life. The nightlight stops the room from falling into complete darkness.

Under the clock, against the wall, on top of the fridge and with a night light

Sneezing

Oh yes, just like us budgies do sneeze. This happens when something is irritating their nasal passages. Anything can set off a sneezing bout. So as soon as a bird starts sneezing, quickly look around to see what is causing it. Off course once the offending cause is located, steps should be taken to stop the sneezing.

In my case I was fortunate to find the cause practically straight away, it was quite obvious. Limpy always flew and landed on my head when I was shaving. As soon as I applied an aftershave he would go into a sneezing fit. This was evident that the fumes were irritating his nasal passages. He would instantly stop sneezing when he either flew away or I had capped the bottle. In a way it was rather funny, me seeing him sneeze. If anything he never suffered from a blocked nose.

If your budgie does have the occasional sneeze that's alright, however if he does start to sneeze carry out a nasal inspection. If you see mucus appearing just above the cere takes him to see a veterinarian. No time to waste, he needs to be checked out.

Stubbornness

The budgerigar is one of the most stubborn creatures on earth. He'll do whatever he wants when he wants to, in his own time. He's ready when he's ready and not when you say so.

Keep this in mind when the time comes to start interacting with him. He plays by his rules not yours. Don't forget that he's also very cautious about any change in everyday life. A creature of habit and structure, he'll accept change on his terms at his own pace.

Temperature

Budgies prefer warm conditions rather than the cold. They are hardy enough to adjust to anything from 0 to 40C but are far more comfortable in the 18 to 30C range. Don't subject them to extremes, unless that's how you live yourself. Once the temperature is becoming uncomfortable to us we tend to switch on the air conditioner. Make sure that the cage isn't directly in front of the chilled air.

Do leave plenty of water preferably in a big enough container for the budgie to not only drink but possibly step in the container itself to cool down. A sign of becoming overheated is when they'll just lift their wings away from their bodies.

When you see that, mist the bird with a fine spray of cool tap water, as often as possible. When carrying out a spraying don't spray directly at the budgie, spray up so that the water falls like light misty rain. If the budgie extends his wings, that's the signal that he's quite hot. That sign is also a welcoming, enjoyable sign. He loves the misting.

Toys

A toy, it's an unusual thing to buy for a bird! Does he need a toy? Does he play with toys?

Well, in actual fact a budgie does play with them. It clearly keeps him occupied throughout the day. He doesn't know it but the activity helps his mental and physical well-being.

Put yourself in his place, imagine being kept in a locked room all day long with nothing to do; you'll climb the wall out of sheer frustration. The same applies to your winged friend.

Out in the wild a budgie who doesn't as yet have a mate will spend most of the day looking for food, preening and having a quick nap or two. Once mated and he or she has chicks it is a case of spending the day looking for food, eating and feeding others. A lot of that time is flying back and forth and he does cover quite a large area.

This activity doesn't give him time to do anything else. In captivity however it is a different story. He's not looking for food, doesn't have to; food it is always there available on a daily basis. As he hasn't any need to look out for any flying or land based predators he slows down, a case of lethargy. Even if there's a possible mate present, he doesn't have to look for her. So he has time on his hands. It is for this reason that toys are introduced.

A few toys to move, push, tear apart, even destroy are ideal to keep him occupied throughout the day. He doesn't know it but these activities help his mental and physical well-being, more so if he's able to fly any distance.

Incidentally, keep in mind that when you introduce a new toy, don't expect the budgie to instantly start playing with it. Remember budgies are suspicious of new things. Just place the toy close by and let him approach it at his own time.

Do make sure that the toy is of an appropriate size. I laughed my head off when a person I knew bought her budgie a two foot high teddy bear. What do you think he was going to do with it? The bird was petrified of it.

Even though both my birds have had the run of the house they still have their toys to keep them occupied. Limpy loved tearing up toilet paper. He enjoyed boring a hole through the roll or tear strips of it. His record much to my amusement and annoyance was totally destroying three rolls in one day. Oz-e thoroughly enjoyed gently pushing a ball against a mirror and banging a plastic ball against a jug.

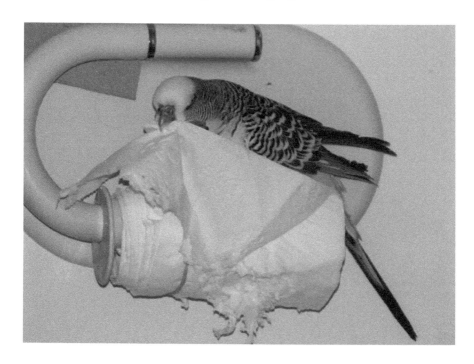

The veterinarian

Your "vet" is your best friend when it comes to looking after your pet's health. The vet understands your budgie more than you do. Veterinarians have dedicated most of their lives looking after similar pets and are able to quickly diagnose and act when your budgie is sick. When it comes to your bird's health never put money ahead. Each bird is unique and is far more important than money.

In my own case I have always taken my budgies to the Burwood Bird & Animal Hospital. I could not recommend highly enough the two avian vets there.

Transporting the budgie

It is quite stressful to the budgie when being transported to the vet. Apart from taking him out of his comfort zone he is being subjected to the unnatural, to him, movement plus experiencing both acceleration and braking and side force movement of the car.

When you return back home he'll instantly fly to his perch and will, for some time remain very quiet. You'll know when he's comfortable again when he starts to softly chirp.

Warning Signs

Within an extremely short period of owning a budgerigar you'll become aware if the bird is sick. The following signs will cause alarm bells to ring.

At first glance, even from a distance a budgie sitting on the cage floor OR showing one or either wing drooping is enough to warrant further investigation.

A discharge from the eyes or nostrils is critical and a change in droppings may be cause for concern (e.g. diarrhea) panic stations (e.g. blood).

There are other signs such as a noticeable increase or loss of appetite, the eyes either partially close or fully closed, a fluffed appearance, weight loss, abdominal distension or other lumps and bumps, lameness, lethargic movements or untidy feathers. Before any of these become worse you should be rushing the budgie to the vet.

Remember a budgerigar is able to mask his illness. Therefore do not make the mistake of saying "we'll see what he's like tomorrow"

This isn't an option. For that bird there might not be a tomorrow.

Whistling

Chirping is one of the ways budgies communicate with each other. In our case not only are we unable to chirp, we do not even understand such a language. We therefore must create a language that in time through repetition and listening we'll be able to communicate with our budgie. Yes it does sound rather a tall order but it is true, it does work.

Start by whistling a simple two tone whistle and start whistling it whenever you're near the budgie or about to enter the room where he is. Be repetitive, whistle it day and night. This is extremely important. As the days turn to weeks whistle the same tune over and over again. If you are unable to whistle make a clicking sound or repeat the same word.

Since you are not going to hurt him then he will in time be able to associate the whistle as a "safe" sound in your presence.

This safe sound comes in very handy when you're very close to him such as replenishing his feed and water or if he is startled. Always whistle when entering the room at night where he can sense someone is there but can't see you. The most important reason of all is when he suddenly wakes up from a night terror. That often heard sound is his reassurance that everything is all right, "do not worry you're safe".

Because he is able to mimic the sound, one day, one special moment when you least expect it he'll repeat it back to you. You could not possibly imagine the joy when you'll hear him repeat the tune. You'll immediately reply and hold your breath waiting for him to repeat it.

Once he has started mimicking that whistle he'll add it to his repertoire of chirps. Every time you enter the room whistle it and most likely he'll whistle it back at you. I say most likely because he plays with his rules not yours. That whistle will become a standard "playback" between you and the bird. One day he'll whistle once or twice, other days he'll keep whistling for quite some time.

Now, on one occasion enter the room and don't whistle, say nothing, ignore him. And this is when he'll contact you. Yes, he'll whistle first because he has gotten so used to hearing your whistle he'll actual wonder why you haven't, so he'll start. Nothing has been said but now the lines of communication have opened more.

Pay close attention to the duration and volume of his whistle. If for example his whistle is at a soft pitch and short duration, you must reply as close to his whistle as possible because if you whistle loudly or over a long duration he will not reply because that's not the way he has learned it.

One day as you're exchanging calls, whistle a different tune. You'll see the budgie suddenly stop whistling, look around and actually tilt his head. It is like suddenly he wants to pay attention, listen to this new tune and learn it.

He will eventually play it back. But he does more than that, in time over a period of months, he'll start to mix even modify the tunes.

As both of you become quite comfortable with the whistle exchange you'll whistle certain tunes which become certain 'commands' I used a two tone whistle as a greeting and for stepping onto my finger. A single short sharp tune is used for the budgie to fly onto my shoulder. I surprised two visitors when, following the appropriate whistle, Limpy flew onto my shoulder; they reckoned that my bird was more responsive that their dog! You'll also learn that his different whistles mean different messages depending on what's happening at the time.

The song "if we could talk to the animals" is quite appropriate. Well believe it or not we can communicate; in this case with one of the most misunderstood birds, the budgerigar.

Yawning

Budgies do yawn. This happens when they are tired or bored. Yep, just like us. But there's also another reason and the only way you'll know the difference is by the circumstances.

Although a budgerigar is quite a social bird there are times when he wants to be left alone. This usually occurs when he's about to settle down for the night. If you approach him at such a time and he opens his beak that's not a sign of yawning, that is a warning sign.

Just like a dog growls to show his displeasure, a budgie may open his beak and keep it open till whoever is annoying him backs away.

When Limpy wanted solitude, as for instance when he was about to go to sleep, he would warn me to stay away by opening his beak. Observing him through the bathroom mirror he closed his beak as soon as I backed away. The funny thing was that as soon as I turned my back to him, he flew onto my shoulder.

Section 3

Budgerigar Interaction

Interaction–the most rewarding of all

We now come to the part where you're going to change the relationship between you and your budgie from a passive to an active one. This is where bonding truly begins. If successful (and there's no reason why it shouldn't be) this relationship is unlike any other. It is extremely rewarding and something that you'll never ever forget.

At the start it isn't easy but as you gain more knowledge on how the budgie reacts to you, plus an increase in your own confidence you'll see improvements in behaviour towards each other. Observing is very important because his behaviour will help you understand him.

Think what you're going to accomplish. Communicating with another person who doesn't speak your language isn't going to be easy. Repetition of hand movement usually is the only way to pass a message across.

You're about to communicate with a budgerigar, it isn't exactly an easy task. This is because

- You have nothing in common.
- He's unable to relate to you.
- Doesn't show any facial features so you do not know whether you're getting through to him.
- Any sudden movement and he'll fly away.

All of these make what seems to be an impossible mission.

Thankfully to help you, you have two advantages on your side, patience and a higher level of intelligence over him.

Oh yes, patience is a must when it comes to interact with your feathered friend. Yet once you start to see your first lesson coming to fruition it becomes so rewarding that there is an overwhelming desire to keep on going.

Yes it takes patience and understanding to bond with a budgie.

From the moment you bring the budgerigar into the household you must at every opportunity spend time with him. Socialization is of paramount importance. It is the first building block of any human/bird relationship. This is the first step to take to start the bonding procedure. Without it, there's not much chance of a relationship forming between the two of you. Even if you do not say a single word to him, even if you totally ignore him you're indirectly showing him that you're safe, you mean him no harm. Just being in his presence is enough for him to take an interest in you. Singing, talking and making a simple sound if you can't whistle is enough to start bridging the gap between you.

Whilst carrying out any activity inside the house keep the budgie close to you. Being on the computer or while watching TV is ideal; in fact, any activity where you're not moving about. By placing the cage next to you, it can, in time, cause him to see you as a strange 'thing' and that although you make strange noises, you aren't dangerous.

In front of the TV, the annoying commercials come in handy because you can turn to look at the budgie and communicate.

Communicate; yes it is by learning a new language, one to which he can relate, you'll be able to understand each other. Observe a dog rounding up sheep. The owner conveys instructions through various whistles.

There are 3 steps to follow:
1. Sound (preferably whistle)
2. Movement
3. Repetition

Sound (preferably whistle)

The first step is to get him used to his surroundings and feeling comfortable by getting used to the sound of your voice. Talk, whistle, and sing, it's all the same to him. From an audio point of view although he can't understand anything it is something that he, in time, will recognise.

A budgie is able to tell the difference in your tone so you need to just relax, this in turn will help him relax. Talk, sing or whistle to him through the cage bars, let him get to know your voice. Proceed very slowly, this is not a race.

Movement

Movement is just as important. A bird is easily frightened. Any movement that he's not familiar with he perceives as a threat and he'll simply take off. He doesn't know where he is going; he's just gaining height to get out of danger. So keep movement down to a minimum. When it comes to moving around him the most important thing to remember is not to make any sudden moves such as rapidly raising your hand or worse doing so from **out of his field of vision**. This is of paramount importance when you start to interact with him. He needs to be shown, that when eventually you're going to let your finger approach him to step on, that such a movement is quite safe. Incidentally when you're very close to a budgie try not to make any loud noises as this has the same effect as sudden movement.

Repetition

Repetition, day in and day out the same act is to be repeated as this is most important. A budgerigar way of understanding is by being shown the same movement over and over again. Eventually it will sink in.

The day will come when the budgie following these three steps, will give you a present -------HIS TRUST. Until you have earned a budgie's trust, no interaction will take place.

Remember and I must keep harping at this; even when you both trust each other the most important thing to keep in mind is that a budgerigar will take off in an instant. It is his self defence behaviour. High speed takes off and flight is his advantage and he will use this at every opportunity. Any sudden movement, even a loud noise (such as a sneeze) will see the budgie take to the air. Do not be disheartened, once he sees that no danger is present he'll relax and you can continue with the current activity.

Under certain circumstances he'll re-trace his steps to see what's happening. His curiosity gets the better of him.

The first physical act of interaction is for the budgie to step on your finger. A reminder, patience is a virtue. A budgie does what he wants to do in his own time and not when you say so.

Oz-e would instantly fly and hide behind the three jugs yet without fail would immediately step out to see what the noise was.

Speaking of trust, it took Oz-e over 5 months before I could get close enough for him to groom my nose. A month earlier he rather casually stepped on my finger.

As every movement made by you looks dangerous to him do not simply move your hand towards him. Start by placing a hand with an extended finger just outside the cage with the idea of slowly over time moving it closer towards him. The very slow movement isn't threatening at all and the bird will get used to the hand.

When you feel that the finger is close enough yet the budgie is neither flying away nor stepping back, briefly pull back your hand. Then, to help him understand that you mean him no harm, keep your hand still, do not move it back towards him.

This is the perfect time to encourage the bird by offering some seed. Budgies thoroughly love millet. Use this love to your advantage. Hold a small shoot or twig of millet and approach the budgie. It is best to hold it in such a way that the tip is as far away from your hand as possible; thus, he doesn't feel threatened.

Before you know it he'll approach and start to eat the seeds. Technically speaking your feathered friend is eating off your hands. Don't expect miracles and although sometimes they do happen with budgies, it is best to continue this over a period of a few days.

Although by now you are already wearing a smile over what you have achieved, do not fret when suddenly, half way through his eating, he instantly flies away. This is expected. A budgie will take this course of action as a defensive act. Although he has excellent vision, while he's busy eating, he has the instinct to fly away from any possibly approaching predators. He'll look around till he's satisfied that he's safe and will return to the feed.

As he becomes more comfortable with your hand close to him, again over a few days, shorten the millet shoot until eventually he's quite close to your finger. This is it, the next step is to place a few seeds in you open palm up and wait. A few moments of indecision and two or three steps later he'll start eating off your hand.

This will definitely place a smile on your face, more so when unable to reach the next seed or two he steps up onto your hand and continue eating. At no time should you ever make a move. Remember, you have a bird that any movement means danger so keep perfectly still.

The next step is to move your hand in a different part of the cage or even try and pull the hand out of the cage. This 'conditioning' helps the budgie not only to continue getting used to your hand but slowly learn to trust you even more. This in turn helps further bond with you.

A treat, I would give some millet spray as soon as Oz-e ate out of the palm of my hand. Not only was he eating out of my hand but he had started to trust me more, I was able to move him away from his 'safe zone'

Clearly food is an ideal motivator during this period of interaction. Even when hungry there will be times when with food present he will not get onto your hand. If he detects any change or if he feels there's danger he'll completely back away. Do not be concerned, he'll come back, just remember, in his own time.

The time will come when you want him to get onto your hand without any food offering. One reason for this is that offering millet spray is all well and good but you must keep in mind that millet spray is fattening so it shouldn't be offered on a daily basis if your bird is prone to putting on weight. It is best to use it as a treat.

So, now comes the time to get the budgie to step onto your finger. By now he has gotten used to your hand. This doesn't mean you can just rush your arm towards him. He doesn't know what you're doing so again approach him from a distance, giving him time to get used to seeing such a large object coming towards him. Slowly, very slowly move a finger towards him. Never make any sudden moves.

Place the finger very close to his chest just above his feet. To him this 'intrusion' is unacceptable thus his first move is to raise his feet and place them where he can see them. So he places them onto the nearest perch, in this case, your finger. It does take time and requires patience. His desire to fly away is still strong so as soon as the bird climbs onto a finger there's also the desire to fly away. And most likely he will. To help stop him from taking off move the finger close enough to nearly touch a mirror. This will cause the bird to start looking at his 'new mate' and he will be so absorbed that he'll forget he's on a human finger. Without realising it he'll accept and will be comfortable being on this new 'perch'.

G'day mate

Patient is a virtue so continue to get him to step up onto your finger till it becomes second nature to him. Just as you slowly introduce the hand with food closer and closer to the budgie, the reverse can now be applied by stepping away from the mirror. It might sound rather unproductive but it is best to get the budgie to step onto your finger in other places. By doing so you are showing the budgie that it is quite safe. From his point of view it strengthens his trust in you. It also comes in handy when you move about the room.

Before you start to train him to step onto your shoulder, now it is the time to teach him a verbal command that he, over time will recognise and obey. As you present your finger for him to step on give a verbal command either in the form of a whistle or a simple short word. Just as he's about to step on the finger say "UP" and as he does praise him by saying something like "Yippee" Keep the words short and sweet, don't say a full sentence. In time the word "UP" will be associated on stepping on your finger. When he begins to land onto the finger on hearing this command, then you can start to step away from him inch by inch. As he gains more trust and confidence he has no hesitation of flying towards you. A step or ten away from you is no big deal to him. The following photo shows Oz-e about to land on my finger having taken off from the top of the cupboards following a command. My commands are not verbal just different whistles.

Coming in for a landing

The next step is to get him to step up on your shoulder. This helps you to free a hand to move about and for him to learn to trust you even more.

Slowly moving your hand towards the shoulder is the way to go. Do not bring the hand too close to the head, give him 'space" Do not crowd him. Whistling, soft talking or gentle singing helps him relax. Remember he's a blink away from flying away if he senses any form of danger. It is going to take time for him to accept your shoulder as a perch. When he finally does step on or lands on your shoulder do not move around. Sit down, try to relax, perhaps start watching TV or read a book. By constantly repeating the action it shows him that it is quite safe to land on the shoulder.

There is an alternative way to get him to stay on your shoulder. By now he's quite comfortable staying on your hand so one day put on a long sleeve shirt, preferable a woollen one. A long sleeve dress shirt is not desirable as it can be slippery. Pull the stretched sleeve very close to the fingers so it wouldn't be a problem for him to accept this strange form of surface and in time will get used to it.

Once you have moved it down far enough for him to step on the next step is to very slowly start to lower your arm. His next course of action is to either fly off or as the tilting becomes extreme he will start to literally climb up. Yes, by using a combination of beak and feet he'll easily make short work of the climb to the top. This is great because not only does he eventually reach the shoulder and level ground but the act of climbing will see him exercising and more importantly keeps him active.

You'll know he has accepted this 'perch' when he starts to groom himself. From then on he'll begin to investigate the new surrounds. Before you know it he'll start to actually groom the ear. A full beard is worth investigating too and will most likely start to pull a single hair to 'test' its strength or simply play with it.

Bonding is certainly alive and well here.

Slowly, so as not to cause the budgie reason to fly away, start to move around the room. Do this at every opportunity. You are teaching him to be able to balance himself as you move about, very similar for him to being on a tree branch. This moving about will in time become an everyday event and will accept it as normal. Yes there will be times when, for whatever his reason, he will fly away back to his perch. If he flies onto a new spot so much the better, he's starting to explore his surroundings.

It will not be long before perching on your shoulder becomes so common that when you enter the room he'll fly onto your shoulder. Once that happens, and believe me it will, you can safely state that you have firmly bonded.

Now, at times slowly move towards the door. You're basically testing him to see whether by approaching the door and that means leaving his normal flight area, he will fly off and return back to his perch.

If he does that's OK, remember he doesn't know what you're doing therefore he'll fly away back onto his perch because there he feels safe. Perform the same manoeuvre again when ready. Sooner or later, once you approach the door frame he'll stay on. When he does remain on the shoulder he's showing you that he trusts you.

Now the idea here, if you so desire, and this helps him to further exercise and stay in far better shape, is to expand his flight area. The time has come to show him other rooms for him to fly to. This also, in turn, shows him which rooms to stay out of.

Slowly while whistling or making any noise that he is now able to recognise and associate with, walk preferably along the corridor to any room that you want him to enter. If you are passing a room that you do not want him to enter, close the door. Repeat this slow walk and then enter the desired room. This procedure shows him where he can fly and he will do so because you're showing the "flight path" in a safe environment.

Continue to show him where he's welcomed and where not. This will not take place in one day. Eventually he will fly off your shoulder or finger and land in a spot that he feels safe. Make a note of this landing zone. Rest assure he will fly there again. Leaving a few seeds will help too. To keep the area clean place a sheet of paper down for his droppings. To further encourage him to fly and land there scatter some seeds. He'll love this as he will forage for the food.

In time a few strategic "eating stations" will see your budgie happily fly around the house.

As he flies about you'll hear the sound of a pair of healthy wings. Some people say, "Big deal." but when the budgie isn't flying it is one sound sadly missed.

Now while observing your budgie flying about, think what you have set out and successfully accomplished. Look back to the day you brought him home. He was frightened, quite stressed from being in a new environment. This resulted in him being very quiet. It took a number of days for him to relax resulting in emitting the first chirp. He spoke to you in his language telling you that he's now relaxed by starting to merrily chirp the day away.

Then from mimicking your whistle to the first time that he didn't back away as you approached him; the first tentative step on your finger; landing on you as you enter his room and finally to the ultimate act of love, his act of regurgitating his food on to your thumb, look what has been achieved.

If for some reason any visitor asks whether your budgie talks or does some sort of trick, you can tell them you didn't get a bird to show off; you got a bird mostly for companionship.

Congratulations, you have bridged the wide gap between a human and a bird. You have successfully communicated and were understood by a bird. You have now completely bonded.

Only one thing can break this bond and when that day comes you will miss him terribly.

But in the meantime ------enjoy his company.

Lightning Source UK Ltd.
Milton Keynes UK
UKHW02f1834260618
324826UK00009B/122/P

9 780994 150912